For those wondering about the number on my book cover, the mystery is solved if you read on!

If you look closely, you will see the digital readout on the vernier calliper that I am holding is 1.618. This number represents the start of the numerical presentation of phi (pronounced fee) and is one letter short of Phil!! (Cue trombone sound.) It is known in some circles as the most beautiful number in the universe and more generally as the 'golden mean/ratio' or 'divine proportion'.

Observed a lot in nature, from sunflowers to sea shells, it closely relates to the Fibonacci sequence, studied over hundreds of years by all the great mathematicians and witnessed in Leonardo Da Vinci's Mona Lisa.

During my time as a furniture maker, I would often use this ratio to work out how big a base would need to be for a table of any given top size.

THE MAN WHO TRIED
to Prove too Much

Philip Hills

Hardie Grant

BOOKS

This book is dedicated to my beautiful wife Melinda
and my two gorgeous daughters Scarlett and Lyla.
Thank you for sharing my life with me.
All my love forever xx

Oh and to all of humanity – I think that covers everyone ☺

Philip Richard Hills
02/09/1971 – 22/07/23

Published in 2023 by Hardie Grant Books an imprint of Hardie Grant Publishing

Hardie Grant Books (Melbourne)
Ground Floor, Building 1, 658 Church Street
Richmond VIC 3121, Australia

Hardie Grant Books (London)
5th and 6th Floors, 52–54 Southwark Street
London SE1 1UN, United Kingdom

www.hardiegrant.com.au

Hardie Grant acknowledges the Traditional Owners of the Country on which
we work, the Wurundjeri People of the Kulin Nation and the Gadigal People of
the Eora Nation, and recognises their continuing connection to the land, waters
and culture. We pay our respects to their Elders past and present.

A catalogue record for this
book is available from the
National Library of Australia

A catalogue record of this book is available from the National Library of Australia.
The Man Who Tried to Prove Too Much
ISBN 9781761441455

Publication commissioned by Courtney Nicholls
Publication managed by Hannah Louey
Edited by Gabriele Conrad
Cover design by Michelle Crowe
Cover photography by Nick Boville
Proofreading by Ariane Durkin
Typeset in Calluna 11/17pt by Cannon Typesetting
Printed in Australia by Griffin Press

The paper this book is printed on is certified against the
Forest Stewardship Council® Standards. Griffin Press holds
chain of custody certification SCS-COC-001185. FSC®
promotes environmentally responsible, socially beneficial
and economically viable management of the world's forests.

Contents

PART ONE: DIAGNOSIS OF A TERMINAL ILLNESS
*I explore what it is to be diagnosed with a terminal illness and
start processing what on earth this all means.*

1	Reflecting on Death	3
2	The Moment My Life and Those around Me Changed Forever	8
3	Dealing with the Realisation	21

PART TWO: MY EARLY YEARS
Where I talk about my early years and you learn a little more about me.

4	Filling the Silence – Being Jimmy Joker and Good at Banter	29
5	He Who Dares, Rodders, He Who Dares	36
6	The Law of Supply & Demand	44
7	Becoming the Storyteller	48

**PART THREE: GOING IT ALONE. GETTING A CAREER.
FINDING COMFORT IN MONEY.**
*When I felt like it was up to me to make my way in the world. A very
basic binary attitude was developed: you were with me or against me –
no shades of grey.*

8	The Great Escape	65
9	When I Slammed into Drive	77
10	Playing with the Big Boys	94

11 The Bright Lights of London's West End and Beyond   112

12 Hong Kong Philly   118

13 Colombia   134

PART FOUR: MOVING OVER TO DOWN UNDER

Seeking out life in paradise which, at the time, I thought was going to be the final piece of the jigsaw.

14 Better Than a Miracle   147

15 Making the Break   165

16 Maizon Hits National TV   189

PART FIVE: WHAT HAVE I LEARNT?

In these last two chapters, I bring you to my more recent years and what I have learnt through the process of writing this book.

17 Right Before My Eyes   207

18 The Burden of Proof   220

Afterword   229

Coming in to land ...   237

Surrender – Melinda's perspective   241

Acknowledgements   247

PART ONE

———ↂ———

DIAGNOSIS OF A TERMINAL ILLNESS

I explore what it is to be diagnosed with a terminal illness and start processing what on earth this all means.

CHAPTER 1

Reflecting on Death

Simple Minds – Alive and Kicking (1985)

In this chapter, I have recently been discharged from hospital and am processing my situation.

I REALISE THAT AS a novice book writer, the title of the first chapter in my first ever book is somewhat confronting for the reader to digest. Please understand this book may seem like it is a book about dying; however, I'd rather like you to see it as a book about living.

Here we are. You, the reader, and me going on this journey together. So, first things first and not wanting to overdo the 'first' as a figure of speech, it's important to explain how I've ended up in this unenviable cul de sac in my life. It's also a scarily accurate description of how I feel and what I'm thinking right now.

My book rather ironically starts very near the end of it in a chronological sense. You join me at the very-soon-to-be age of 50. The date is mid-July 2021 and I'm back at my home in Rozelle, Sydney, computer out and at my desk following a trip to hospital for seven days that began only a week or so earlier. This was when I was first diagnosed with terminal brain cancer, following a shock MRI scan that landed me in hospital – don't pass go, do not collect $200 – go straight to hospital. This will be covered in the next chapter. I'm in post-operation recovery mode after a brain biopsy and routine stay in ICU. My head is in a storm. A whirlwind of thoughts that are mostly of a confused nature, trying to make some sense of how I ended up in a predicament that only as little as a few weeks ago was a scenario that would have been my worst nightmare.

Every swallow at this stage causes me pain. My throat is hurting from the intubation that was required to keep me breathing while the craniotomy was performed and they removed a small walnut-sized piece of my brain containing a tumour. I've never been a fan of ice cream but uniquely found myself at the supermarket on the day after my discharge, staring at the freezer section deciding which flavour ice cream to buy. I went with Ben & Jerry's choc chip. Wow, it's good. Should be called nice cream. My upper jaw hurts too as they went in to get the walnut through my jaw muscles. I also get a tightness all around my shoulders and neck, which is possibly from the fact that they had to go through the barrier that surrounds the brain and spinal cord called the dura mater.

Anyway, back to my thoughts of what my new life will look like and consist of, now that the realisation and reality are laid bare and the swarm of specialists, doctors, nurses, porters and the people who deliver my in-room meals are no longer keeping me occupied. It's sobering stuff, that's for sure. Especially coming from a guy that hasn't touched alcohol by choice for almost six months.

I've never been a person to think about death. I love music as will be evidenced by song titles introducing each chapter. I actually chose lyrics as well, but of course they are covered by copyright; however, I adapted a set of lyrics to fit one of the latter chapters. Given this lifelong love of music, I've had the odd moment where in the past I've considered what song I would like to be played at my funeral (oh, the irony), but that's as far as it ever went. Which is just as well, as that song has changed many times.

Those dark places I've heard one can go that inhabit the deepest recesses of the brain have never featured heavily, if at all, in my thoughts, no matter what my personal situation has been.

For me life is about living, surviving and thriving, and even entertaining the notion it could or should end prematurely is just worlds away from my everyday thinking. Hence the song title introducing this chapter.

I can safely say I've never had the impulse, or had to control the impulse, to jump over the railing of a tall building, step in front of a bus or train, slug a bottle of whiskey or take pills ... that's just not even a bit of me. Thankfully for my family and those close to me and you, the reader, I've chosen to write this book instead to express myself and help with the situation.

I heard an incredible statistic a while ago that in Australia one person every two days does get that suicide impulse and ends their life stuck to the front of a train.

So, as I sit here typing this with the recently diagnosed Grade 4 Glioblastoma – that was removed, resected being the fancy medical term, but nonetheless still typically carries a dire prognosis (sometimes months, not years) – my thoughts are returning to death all too often.

However, instead of being consumed and confused by the finality of it all, I'm finding there is something quite calming and liberating and with it a strange sense of freedom that comes from knowing how I will peg out.

Nothing left to prove and no more expectations. The first part of that sentence is a nod in part to the title of the book – *The Man Who Tried to Prove Too Much*.

Not so much of a death sentence, more of a life sentence ... or, more accurately, a life lesson.

Many clichés can be used to dull the realisation of the impending outcome and justify it to myself.

Life causes death, no one gets outta here alive, bad things happen to good people, only the good die young, the brighter the light – the shorter it burns ... the list is long, even the Queen reflecting on the death of her husband Prince Phillip said, 'No one lives forever.' I'm no royal watcher but I think that's probably the best thing I've ever heard her say. From an individual who's lived most of his life by replying with contrived platitudes, I feel these one-liners underplay the deeper meaning of the lesson on offer from the universe, right here, right now – being from Brighton I had to drop in a Fatboy music reference.

This is my story, a story of true stories and an insight into how I came to feel compelled to tell it. They are for the most part 100 per cent accurate but with the unrelenting passage of time and notwithstanding some are nearly 40-odd years old, some minor details may be slightly out. It is not, however, in any way deliberate to make the stories juicier, embellish them for the purpose of making them more palatable for you, the reader, or for me writing to indulge my fantasy in some make-believe.

For as long back as I can remember, I always imagined that this life was not the singular event we sometimes believe it to be ... I would always joke that in a parallel universe I would be a racing car driver or professional snowboarder, so maybe that life in the parallel universe is not parallel but sequential ... either in the past or the future ... or both ... see where I'm going here?

You may be forgiven for thinking that because I'm now about to be flicked off the chessboard, my views into the circle of life are just me having a quid each way bet on the future and that's fair enough, but if you had asked me 10 or 20 or even 30 years ago what my beliefs were – spiritual, religious, etc., – I would have said I aligned to a broad Buddhist way of thinking. I couldn't have told you in any great detail how it worked and I wasn't sure back then if rapists, murderers or paedophiles came back as cockroaches or came back as anything, but what I couldn't ever imagine is anyone getting away with wrongdoing – roughly this translates to karma, I think.

As you read further you will learn that poor choices come in many forms other than just my narrow definition of murderers, etc.

Talking of all this ... who's in charge of the future and where do I find their number? As I broaden and deepen my knowledge into a lot of things it turns out I already have it ... it's my number and I'm in charge of my future. That's the good news, the bad news ... it's just a shame I didn't give myself a call many, many years ago.

CHAPTER 2

The Moment My Life and Those around Me Changed Forever

Oasis – Lyla (2010)*

In this chapter I go into a little more detail about the lead up to my hospital admission.

I T WAS THE start of the winter school holidays along with the start of yet another Covid lockdown. We thought it was just going to be an isolated lockdown in the Eastern Suburbs of Sydney where the girls live half of the time with their mother, Lauren. We live in Balmain, in the Inner West of Sydney – we thought we had escaped the lockdown and toyed with the idea of keeping the girls over our side so that they could have a bit more freedom in their school holidays. Didn't have to worry too much about that as the very next

---

* Yes, my daughter is named after the Oasis track. Not as in a I've got Oasis images tattooed all over my back, arms and neck kind of way. It's a great track, that's for sure, but it's also a lovely name and choosing a name for your child is a minefield to navigate. Both mother and father have to agree. Then make sure no other friends/family members have it. It was a song (like all Oasis songs) I played regularly and we both liked it, it wasn't a common name, so we chose it.

day they locked down the entire city and surrounds. I had started to feel some weird things occurring and I had a treatment session on my neck and shoulders as these areas had been getting tighter and tighter lately. Melinda, my partner at the time and now my wife, just so happens to be a physiotherapist and her clinic was around the corner. It was the first day of yet another total lockdown for Covid. A surreal time as pubs and restaurants fell silent and offered up their takeaway services. The next day we went for a bike ride. Me on my remodelled BMX bike that I had restored in the last lockdown, right down to the spray painting in a beautiful electric blue, dice on the rims and stickers to complete. I'll preface what happened next in that, yes, I rode BMX bikes as a kid and rebuilt the BMX as a lockdown project so I could ride with Scarlett, my eldest, who had just taken up riding. She could never understand why at the time I just didn't buy one already made but now I think she and all my family and friends understand that is not the Philip Hills way – where is the fun in that? Forever looking for the next creative project! Back to my riding history, I was a natural runner and went to the gym for strength, stretch and core work a few times a week ... I was not a bike rider. Melinda on the other hand rides a racing bike weekly and has done since ... day dot, it would seem. Anyway, off we went on one of her usual routes. I was much slower on my BMX to her racer, which was to be expected but what was not expected was the level of fatigue in my muscles. I'm quite lithe and can usually apply myself to anything I try so this was a bit weird. Melinda waited patiently at the top of each hill as I gradually made my way up. Balmain is hilly and my bike had no gears so that was explainable but again after the ride I was really tired and especially so in my legs. This lasted for two weeks, so much so that on a long walk we decided to do around Callan Park – a beautiful space on the harbour near where we live – Melinda actually stopped at the top of some rocks and said, 'What is wrong with you? You are walking like an old man and you are dragging your right leg.' Melinda notices everything! A good thing and a bad thing, depending on the moment. We kept on blaming the bike ride but really, after two weeks? Then other things started happening ...

So I have two young daughters, Scarlett and Lyla, who over the years have made me play a number of made-up games with them. I'm not talking about the bog-standard hide and seek or catch but those where only the two of you know the rules and to anyone else the rules and roles of each person would seem complicated and confusing. I'm sure, like many parents, there are some of those games that fill you with existential dread whenever they are suggested or as is the case of 'schools' that I play with Lyla, my youngest, it is a happy and relaxed affair that gives us a chance to enjoy each other's company and while away a few hours of a weekend afternoon.

The game 'schools' is really quite simple, unlike school, and involves Lyla setting up a whiteboard or chalkboard on her desk (she's very proud of her double-sided writing apparatus given to her by Nana) and assuming the role of a schoolteacher. I have to play the role of student and will be given a series of maths, spelling or art assignments to complete. Just like every other time I've prepared myself to play the game, I made myself a cup of tea, got comfy on her bed and waited for the tasks to be given to me.

On this particular Sunday, first up was writing and Lyla asked me to write a sentence about what I did that weekend. Dutifully she handed me the notebook that is imperative I use for this subject and when I asked her for a pen it was efficiently presented to me, so there was no chance of me not completing my work.

This time, however, it was not like every other time and as I started to write the few lines I normally put together for this topic, the outcome was very different in terms of my ability to write.

My fingers felt enormous and I struggled to control the tip and accurately judge the distance between nib and paper. From further research into my condition a lot of people say it's like trying to do things with a ski glove on … and looking back that's exactly how it felt. I changed my grip, which felt like my hand was just regaining the feeling from pins and needles, and concentrated really hard to get the words looking intelligible – Lyla is a tough taskmaster and I didn't want to get marked down for my poor handwriting skills which, ironically, I was always hounding her for whenever I helped with her homework.

I struggled through the exercise and made a complete dog's dinner of my writing and a mental note to myself that I should get my shoulder looked at as it felt like a trapped nerve or tightness in a muscle. As mentioned earlier, my beautiful partner Mel is a physio-therapist and I'm fairly confident I wouldn't still have the full use of my limbs had we not met when we did … I've had lots of issues with my shoulders over the years due to overzealous attempts of tricks on snowboards and skateboards etc., so I didn't really give it a second thought.

From an energetic point of view, shoulder issues are burdens … I had missed the memo on that one.

The rest of a lovely Sunday passed without incident and on Monday both my daughters unilaterally decided we were having bacon and egg rolls for lunch; naturally, there was no objection forthcoming from me.

Another game we enjoy is usually played when walking home from our regular Friday night trip to the pub or restaurant. This is more family fun (though Mel has never been a big fan of it and I'm not sure exactly why) and involves hiding behind a car if you are the first one to turn into the street and jump out on the other three to scare them.

So, there we were, three of us walking back from the café and I find myself first round the turn. Great, I think, as I look back and see Scarlett and Lyla happily clutching brown paper bags with their beautiful greasy contents, oblivious to what I'm planning.

It's a road I know well and there was no traffic around and I bolted a couple of car lengths down the middle of the road and went to nestle up behind the front wing of the car so I could see them coming through the glass canopy of the car's body, ready for a warrior-style charge.

Except it didn't go down like that at all. What went down like a sack of wet cement was me onto deck as I scrambled to balance myself against the car while my legs totally gave way under me. If anyone had been watching, what they would have witnessed was what looked like one of those marathon runners as they hit that point of complete and utter exhaustion and pin-ball left and right across the track until, after what seems like an eternity, finally the predetermined outcome arrives and despite their best efforts, they collapse in a twisted, tangled wreckage.

As I sat there, covered in the contents of my roll, the girls came into view, but I was so stunned by what just happened the warrior in me failed to fire up and there was no roar from behind the car. They thought it was hilarious, of course, though none of us could possibly have foreseen the seriousness of what had just occurred.

The rest of the day (Monday) passed without incident. By now the 'notes to self' were starting to pile up but, as is the case with family life, the show must go on and I was feeling otherwise well in myself.

I generally consider myself to have a good internal gyroscope and have never struggled with difficult sports that require coordination of my body as well as having good hand to eye coordination. I would be lying if I said I wasn't starting to take seriously these notes to self that were piling up, when I went up the stairs from my garage at a fairly rapid clip, only to round the top corner where we have a curtain that we draw in winter to keep the cold air from the basement out of the house, and totally stacked it. I blew through the curtain like a bull at a matador's cape in an arena and unceremoniously faceplanted into the dishwasher whilst emptying the dregs of my takeaway coffee all over myself. It was now Tuesday.

In fact, about a week earlier, an out-of character event happened that looking back was the precursor to all of these singular events. I was on a zoom call with my APAC team late on a Monday afternoon. I was hotspotting on my phone and suddenly needed my charger that was upstairs. I raced up and back down with it and, whilst rounding the hall corner to the office (aka the girls' bedroom), came to the mat on the floor by the front door. I knew it was there but instead of stepping on it and sliding along like Aladdin on his magic carpet, I totally mugged it and went bouncing off the wall in the hall. Within seconds I had regained my balance, so I jumped back on the call and thought nothing more of it until recollecting these events later.

By the end of Wednesday there would be no doubt things were taking a very serious turn for the worse when, still feeling otherwise well in myself, I had dinner with the family, got the girls' baths done and dinner cleared away, then went for my evening shower.

As I stood under the more soothing than normal cascade of water from the shower head, a quite astonishing thing happened. A memory from years ago entered my head with some accompanying music and a strange smell. Then it hit: a wave of nausea unlike anything I've had the displeasure to experience – and believe me I've pushed my body to some ungodly limits in the past.

In most cases, when you feel sick – or at least as sick as I felt at that point – the only next possible outcome is to chunder. Except it never came and as is usual when you hug the porcelain and you feel like the devil has come for you, throwing up releases you from the feeling and you go about your way. Except there was no vomiting, only more waves of nausea that lasted for 10 minutes at a time.

I eventually went downstairs and told Mel what happened. We put the girls to bed as usual and I got ready for bed feeling significantly better than I did an hour earlier.

I'd had my first Pfizer jab a few days before so some of the symptoms like nausea and aching limbs could be directly attributable to that if you read the health advice. I drifted off to sleep without problems or pain medication but then a ticking time-bomb went off ... in my brain.

I awoke around 1am with the mother of all headaches. Again, like the nausea only a few hours earlier, this felt different. Ridiculously painful but unlike most headaches, this time I could feel it was coming from deep inside my brain. If you've ever done poppers or amyl and been a bit greedy, you'll be getting somewhere close to what this felt like, only the pain continued to build.

I'm not generally a sick person and have been lucky that ill health has never featured strongly in my life, so when Mel saw me frantically rubbing my head and sitting up looking for help in whatever form I could find it, she took my condition seriously.

Nurofen was taken but it didn't really touch the sides as you expect pain relief to work quite quickly. Panadol followed half an hour to an hour later and again no let-up in the pain, so we made the call to get an ambulance. They promptly arrived, took my vitals which were all good, we had a chat about my symptoms and as the painkillers were now kicking in, they suggested it could be migraine. But when we told them about the other weird but somehow linked symptoms, they thought I should jump in the ambulance with them and go to hospital.

I still hadn't thrown up or emptied my bowels and after a brief discussion and knowing I had to do the school run with Lyla, I declined the offer but heeded their advice to see my GP urgently.

It's important to say here that there can be absolutely no criticism of the paramedics on that night with respect to the eventual diagnosis and nothing would have played out any differently if they had bound and gagged me and thrown me in the back of the ambo there and then.

I drifted off to sleep, awoke at my normal time feeling 100 per cent better, got Lyla ready for school and headed off, all the while calling my GP and booking an appointment. It was now Thursday.

As we were driving to school, the song, the image and smell returned along with another overwhelming wave of nausea. I commented to Lyla that I would have to open the window and to also prepare for Dad to do a sudden stop where I would likely vomit on the side of the road. She found it hilarious, of course, and duly reminded me of the time I threw up on my white trainers after getting out the taxi following a rather large drinking session when she couldn't have been any more than four ... kids say the funniest things, don't they!

In the end we didn't have to stop, and I dropped her at school then went on to my GP.

I really wasn't feeling too crash hot in the GP clinic and asked the receptionist for a sick bag, which was similar to an aeroplane one, and I was asked to take a seat in an isolation area as they were clearly concerned about me mixing with other patients. Dr Brittain saw me straight away and I described what had happened holus bolus. He took some vitals, shone a torch in my eyes and agreed with the ambos that I should get an MRI without delay. He gave a me a referral and, as usual, I used comedy to diffuse the situation by saying, 'Will I live, doc?' I can't recall his reply or if there was even one from a line he's probably heard two million times too many.

I called Spectrum Imaging later and got an appointment for the following day, which was Friday. The rest of the day was uneventful, school pick-up went without a hitch ... I picked Scarlett up from Lauren (the girl's biological mother) and they all joked about the sick bag I was firmly clutching and refusing to let go of. Lauren would later tell me I looked very grey during that pick-up; I was actually feeling a lot better but did say to her that I knew something wasn't quite right. In the years of understating my statements that would be the gold medal winner. A personality trait of mine is that I tend to look on the positive side of things a little too eagerly and don't like to communicate my deepest feelings ... Well, we weren't going to have to wait too long for Dad to really show his true feelings. I'm not sure where this reaction to letting people see the real me comes from but by the end of this book, I'm pretty sure I'll have a better idea.

I was really achy in my legs and that night I decided to use the girls' bathroom and actually have a hot bath. What is it with Englishmen and their baths??

Again, the warm water felt more soothing than normal and Mel, Lyla and Scarlett all gathered around in the bathroom and administered Epsom salts and rubbed my weary limbs.

I went to sleep that night terrified I would again be woken by the mother of all headaches. In fact, my brain was still hurting from the previous night but it just felt bruised rather than a headache per se ... it was weird.

The night went without incidence. I woke as usual, took Lyla to school (Scarlett was home-schooling because of Covid lockdowns) and planned my day around the MRI. The scan process was uneventful and I didn't even feel unduly concerned, lying in the tube as they injected the dye and the machine clunked and bumped its way through the program. I hopped up off the table after 15 minutes and left Spectrum clutching my scans and even went via my GP to book a follow-up appointment.

I felt pleased with myself. I was on top of it all and taking it all seriously for once in my life. I needn't have bothered as the universe, or should I say Spectrum Imaging, were a few steps ahead of me.

I was waiting to pick Lyla up from school just before 3pm when I spotted a missed call and voicemail (VM) from my GP. I was juggling work calls so let it go through to the VM keeper, but then saw he was calling again. I took it and his first words to me were:

'Phil, Dr Brittain here. Did you get my message? I've just got your scans and they're very concerning. The radiologist has looked at them and it's looking like glioma. Get yourself straight to A&E but choose a hospital near where you live as you'll be there a while.'

I'm not sure he said get your affairs in order or get plans in order, but he finished the call with a 'good luck'.

It was as blunt as it was direct. No judgement though.

The only other times in my life when I've been on the receiving end of some potentially devastating news from a health professional was when Lyla was diagnosed with epilepsy at less than 12 months and Scarlett had a hole in her heart shortly after birth.

Both incredible stories, which I am forever indebted to the Australian health system for and that reconfirmed my faith that miracles can happen.

One of the reasons I like playing schools with Lyla is because she loves being the teacher and is adamant (or as adamant as any 9-year-old can be) that she will become a teacher one day.

I've always possessed a deep admiration for doctors, nurses, charity workers and teachers. They are professions I've always had respect for because I know I simply couldn't do those kinds of caring roles. (I've mostly worked in corporate roles where my personal outcome and that of my company is the priority.) Perhaps when I get my next go around, instead of being a racing driver or pro snowboarder I could come back and be a little more help to humanity than my endeavours as a salesman – albeit a very good salesman. Along the way I've picked up the noble art of the self-deprecating sense of humour and I would often joke that if I was a swimming pool, I'd be so shallow you'd have to be careful when you dived in not to hit your head. Perhaps I could set up a specialist industry selling advice for humanity? Or is that an oxymoron?

I don't critique those working in the health system ever. I've always worked in private enterprise, both at multinational corporation and small-to-medium business level, mainly in commercial roles where all my decision making, comments or conversations have been about how to add revenue to a company's bottom line or my own commission cheque. I just can't imagine saying things in my professional life that are about the subject of life and death. I have to screw up the courage sometimes just to tell my clients there has been a yearly price increase.

Reminds me a bit of that famous saying of English football manager Bill Shankly. This may not be the exact transcript, but when talking to a journo about a recent football game he remarked something like, 'Some people think football is a matter of life and death ... It's more important than that.'

You could swap some words around for a salesperson:

'Your target isn't a matter of life and death. It's more important than that.'

What followed was arriving home with Lyla to Melinda and Scarlett. I had called Melinda earlier of course, so both knew what was going on. Lyla, unaware of the gravity, knew I was going to hospital and brought down the photo we had on our set of drawers in our bedroom upstairs of me, Scarlett and Lyla many years ago. It is a beautiful photo and she thought that it might provide comfort for Melinda. Nana and Pa (Mel's parents) came over to get the girls – they were free on this particular Friday night as we were supposed to all be going down to theirs for dinner to celebrate Scarlett's birthday, which was on Sunday. It was one of those moments when everyone had fear in their eyes and under hushed tones spoke about what was happening next.

In keeping with Dr Brittain's advice – choose somewhere close – Melinda drove me to Royal Prince Albert Hospital (RPAH) in Camperdown, Sydney, only 15 minutes' drive away. It was a drive into the unknown and where Melinda would be leaving me for the evening as Covid restrictions meant that she could not come in with me. In I went with my briefcase, in my work clothes and having nurses attend to me straight away while I was still attending to work calls. Melinda reflected to me later that it was the hardest thing that she has ever had to do. To me it was surreal – putting one foot in front of the other, but my optimism was still intact. Until of course, when sat in one of the consulting rooms and the neurosurgeon's register flipped up the scans onto the lightboard and said, 'Well, there is definitely a mass showing up on the scans as well as numerous other sites' and in her commanding voice followed up with, 'Phil, I'm afraid it doesn't look good.'

Looking back as I edit these early chapters I wrote, I now know this would be the start of nearly a whole year of treatment including surgery, whole brain radiation, 10 courses of chemotherapy including the first course of daily chemo for six weeks, nine weeks in hospital over two admissions and coming out needing a wheelchair to mobilise, close to 24-hour care initially and learning how to walk and talk again. There is obviously much more detail to go into here and I will leave that to Melinda at the end of my book to fill you in as I admit my memory of this time is hazy ... thank goodness! Luckily, when the brain is faced with trauma it filters out some of the worst moments.

CHAPTER 3

———❦———

Dealing with the Realisation

Death in Vegas – Scorpio Rising (2002)

Where I talk about the origins of this book and start to piece the puzzle of my predicament together.

IT WAS NEVER a life goal to write a book. However, a close friend of mine who has known me since I was a teenager was teasing me recently to write it.

When I was in hospital the thoughts that would occupy my mind seemed to regularly refocus on the bigger picture of life and why we are here, and when someone who has given me much healing and counsel recently also suggested it, it felt true to devote time to it.

Another major influence is my beautiful wife Mel who would often sit and listen slack-jawed and occasionally yawning, along with the words 'yes Philip, heard this one before' to all my various tales and stories over the years and so, with my recent diagnosis there may be stories that would never get told again and we just couldn't let a situation like that occur, could we? So the time seemed as good as any to link them all together.

If you have ever felt compelled to write a book and I hope this energises many readers to attempt it, the questions that need to get posed are: 'Why did you write it?', 'What experiences are derived from it?' and 'How does your experience shape your outlook?'

The understanding of how it benefits both myself and others will hopefully not be underestimated. Those benefits for me are part of my healing process; how I got to be in this predicament and how do I make peace with it.

From a personal point of view, it could be summed up quite succinctly with the following description:

'It was never meant to be a commercial success. It was written to be a way of describing times and places in my life so that those I love could reflect back on my final years and learn more about me than they would if I was still alive. And for me to learn more about me for that matter. It's not about leaving a legacy and have loved ones gather round a paperback effigy of me every night. It's about the healing process this book brings to my life, so whether this is a book they carry around with them every day that never leaves their side or just makes its use in life as a 200-page paperweight, I'm not overly concerned.

Sure, if it turns into a *New York Times* bestseller and provides my family with financial security, then I won't look that gift horse in the mouth either.'

So, let's take a deep dive into the past and see what lessons can be learnt from it and understand why something so pivotal as this diagnosis can crystallise one's thoughts and actions to make clear what was not deemed so important previously. I lived a life in the fast lane, in fact I built my own lane. My way or the highway.

How is it that a man who's never cried once in his entire adult life is now reduced to tears a couple of times a day?

My disease is seemingly totally random and does not discriminate – male, female, all ages – no lifestyle choices, accidents or poor diets are to blame. When I was in hospital the person who has provided much counsel in my life recently suggested I look a little deeper at the bigger picture and take the next step of lifting the veil on why we get sick. A phrase I'd heard but never really understood –

'The action of lifting or removing a veil; (figurative) the exposing of something previously unknown or not generally discussed.'

Or

'To divulge, explain, or reveal something that was previously a secret.'

As my oncologist said to me, I just drew the short straw. Incredibly, one person a week presents with this type of cancer (that I'd never heard of prior, but then I don't spend any of my spare time checking peer-reviewed articles and medical journals much) at the Chris O'Brien Lifehouse in the Inner West of Sydney alone, so there must be a disproportionate number of short straws out there.

Is there any way to avoid this? Well, no is the short and easy answer. I'm going to go into a bit of medical lesson stuff now but please do hang in here as it is all good background information. They do know from longitudinal studies that for cancers like breast and bowel early intervention is critical and linked to survival rates. That early intervention could be either scans or physical examinations. Since brain cancers are only really detectable by MRIs, the logical thing to do would be to scan people. But who do you scan? Since the cancer does not discriminate on age, sex, etc. that leaves a huge swathe of the population to be checked. All men and women from the age of say 40 plus. You would need to do these scans every six months. Why six months? Well, it's such an aggressive form of cancer that, if you had scans in January then you would need to repeat them in July, otherwise, if it was a grade 4 and unless it was removed as soon as it gave an indication it was there, you would be dead before you took your next six-month scan. The load on the health system would be enormous. It's a big process having an MRI and involves a lot of specialists. The machines themselves aren't exactly plentiful nor cheap. It's not like doing a blood test.

I recently celebrated my 50th birthday whilst in hospital and given this wasn't in any way self-inflicted, what other explanation could there be?

If it was written in the stars that I was going to get it ... why now?

Age is a factor in that the older you are, statistically you are more prone to getting it. Every day I woke I took a straw until one day, as the number of straws became less and less, I finally picked the wrong one. People in their teens, 20s and 30s get glioma. I could have picked the wrong straw five, 10 or even 20 years ago ... you could say it was always going to happen, eventually. There is no real way of knowing when the DNA from one tiny cell in my brain copied to the next and was out by just a fraction – bit like writing down a phone number and getting a digit wrong – and the cancer train left the station. The brain is a superhighway of neural pathways and blood vessels and any incorrect coding moves very fast. In my case it could be hypothesised that around two years ago, this coding got corrupted and a low-grade glioma was formed and that around two to three months before I was diagnosed an area switched into hyper-speed and went berserk to create a grade 4 glioma or, as it is known medically, a GBM (glioblastoma multiforme). Low-grade gliomas invariably turn high grade at some point, so they are impossible to cure. Even with surgery and full resection the tentacles they leave through our brain mean full removal is all but impossible. Removing large portions of the brain like other organs is just not an option.

So why now? I was the healthiest I had ever been, had given up alcohol, caffeine and sugar. Had low levels of stress in my life, a beautiful partner, two wonderful daughters, a great job, one might even say my dream job, working for a multi-national high-end design company ... everything to live for, you might say.

Death in Vegas put it perfectly in their epic *Scorpio Rising*, sung by Liam Gallagher:

"I saw my life before me but now I'm blind."

Lift the veil though and that blindness disappears and perhaps what has got me to this point wasn't quite the true representation of who Phil really is. A life of projection and control that wasn't sustainable and given that my house was now well and truly in order it was time to start work on the most important job of my life. *A life of true purpose and service to humanity.*

I've been a very motivated individual my whole life. I've moved jobs regularly, travelled the world for both work and pleasure, become a citizen of Australia and started a business here, purchased multiple properties along the way, had two beautiful daughters, left that long-term relationship as it was clear neither of us were happy. Found love again in another long-term relationship, all the time actively building my career and supporting my children by doing and contributing at the very least my fair share along the way.

This is a perfect opportunity to introduce the 'feather duster, brick and bus' analogy that I'll refer to at different points throughout the book. I've come to understand that life is invariably dotted with those 'sliding door' moments. This phrase is taken from the famous movie, not surprisingly called *Sliding Doors*. The premise being that at any point we can make a different decision that drastically alters the path of our life; the universe, the multiverse etc., whatever your belief system is, gives you a nudge to get your attention and/ or stop the momentum which you are moving in. This nudge can come in the form of a feather duster for minor deviations, a brick to seriously get your attention and finally the bus when the other two haven't had the desired result. I have had plenty of feather duster moments which I dusted off, many a dodged brick as well as those that have landed which you will read about in the coming pages and, of course, I have just been hit by the bus, the meaning of which I am coming to understand more and more and no doubt will furthermore as the book unfolds.

So, there we have it, I am writing this with a backdrop of incurable brain cancer. Just to add another mode of transport to the analogy, you can say the cancer train has left the station and it will continue until it collides into the buffer stops at the end of the main line. The trick now is to ensure that where possible that collision is just a small crash and not a complete train wreck. With a couple of lucky breaks along the way this may just be possible. Only time will tell. My job now is to surrender to the healing the cancer offers and learn to let go of the past and be present to respond to whatever I need to do to prepare myself for the future and the next.

PART TWO

MY EARLY YEARS

*Where I talk about my early years and you learn
a little more about me.*

———⚬———

Filling the Silence – Being Jimmy Joker and Good at Banter

Depeche Mode – Enjoy the Silence (1990)

*So here you go, a window into my world of life, both family and
personal. That's a pretty good start already, so let's now take
a look at my life many decades ago before annoying but much
needed (as we will discover) things like cancer got in the way.
We'll see where and how I grew up so you can get a full idea of
what family life consisted of.*

Growing up in England on the southeast coast back in the 70s
was a carefree and wide-ranging experience. I lived in a small
satellite town called Shoreham-by-Sea, about seven miles outside of
Brighton, the main town along the coast that will be the location for
some of the stories you will read in due course. You may even have
heard of Brighton already, as it's a much spoken about city due to
its proximity to London. It's a big destination for holiday makers.
It also has a thriving culture and arts scene with a polytechnic and
university there. Having a premiership football team also gets you
noticed on the map. Though it wasn't all this way. Brighton became

a city much later on and much, much later it became colloquially known as London-by-Sea as residents from the capital cottoned on to the fact Brighton was only an hour away by train, which was less time than it could take you to get from the outskirts of London to central stations like Kings Cross etc. You then got the benefits of city life with access to the country life of the South Downs on your doorstep. Best of both worlds. Shoreham-by-Sea was pretty quiet but did have great access to the South Downs. Entertainment was in short supply, so you had to make your own fun. There was no cinema or swimming pool. The fair came to town once a year.

Me and my mates, all of whom lived in my street or the next one, went to the same school. I had a good circle of friends and we were either out on our bikes or I could be found at one of their houses. Most of us had a good-sized back garden where football was most often played and if we weren't doing that we were out burning or destroying stuff. It was a good fun childhood but very soon I started to get restless. Suburbia had its limitations and I was starting to bump up against them. As soon as I was old enough, bunking the train to Brighton was routine for visits to the skate park or other entertainment. Though they had built a BMX track in Shoreham by then, the genie was out of the bottle for me and Brighton was where it was at. Meanwhile, back on the home front the week followed a pretty standard routine that I can't remember ever being broken. School Monday to Friday obviously, supermarket shop Thursday evening, followed by Chinese takeaway. There was swimming one night a week but I can't recall when. This meant a trip to Hove, about three miles away. The swimming pool was cold and dirty, so it hardly seemed like a treat. I've never had a problem with most sports but even today I'm a very average swimmer as I disliked that pool so much and never got the enthusiasm up to learn properly. Oh, and there was athletics on a Monday and Thursday evening at a cold and draughty hall that might have even been a theatre on other nights as we had to move the seats when we got there. Cubs and Scouts also featured heavily in evening routines and being fast and agile I was picked for most games without hesitation which was a relief. I've been fortunate that I've never been that poor fellow left at the end when all the choices have been called out. I can't imagine how spirit-crushing that would feel.

So, it was all pretty routine day in day out and something just didn't sit right with me. The level of mediocrity my family seemed comfortable to settle for just wasn't for me. I very much felt like the odd one out. When the time came for me and my friends to get driving licences, I was straight on the road to Brighton. I had an old Triumph Herald convertible as my first car that I bought with money given to me by an inheritance from a distant relative when I couldn't have been more than 10 years old. It wasn't a huge amount but neither were clapped-out classic cars then. It was a lovely old car and my classic car itch got a good scratching from it. I would load up the stereo with tunes and go driving with the roof down on cold evenings, wrapped in a big woollen jumper and just lap the streets of Brighton, from along the seafront through the town up over the hill towards Devil's Dyke, taking in the sights and sounds of the city and all it promised to offer. I was looking to escape from a young age as something to focus on and escapism was the perfect tonic.

All in all, pretty average, all pretty normal but an overriding feeling I can recall growing up in our house at, say, around 10 years old that it was all very quiet. It was all very nice and it seemed too normal, too unreal. There was no debate, either rigorous or lively, everything had its place: everything in its place and a place for everything, I think the saying goes. Other than the sound of Dad when he was working on the house or in the garden (which was very often), there wasn't any background chatter to speak of and music was rarely played though we had a record player that I seem to remember had a built-in radio. It wasn't on much either, if ever. On the positive side, arguments were all but non-existent which in a number of ways was a double-edged sword as I would actively avoid confrontation later in life because I wasn't equipped to deal with it and had no idea about conflict resolution. I never heard the word 'sorry' in my house – ever!

This is probably what leads me to sugar-coat everything in the vain hope a disagreement can be avoided.

I'm going to pause before I write this sentence ... but it felt like it was a place for us as a family to live with each other but not as a family to love each other.

We had a good-quality colour TV, but it wasn't remote control for many years, and we didn't have a VCR until much later.

Dinner times and larger extended family events were sombre affairs where no one really interacted or engaged with each other apart from the basic pleasantries. For some unknown reason I always felt compelled to intervene and took it upon myself to start the conversations. I have no idea what the topics were, looking back, but I tried to make them relevant to whichever family member I had decided needed entertaining and saving from the spirit-crushing boredom.

The toughest family get-togethers that were the trickiest to negotiate were when both sets of grandparents were invited.

Despite both sides of the family living in a small cul de sac where they were next-door neighbours when Mum and Dad were young, there seemed to be an unnecessary rivalry between them. There could be no doubt they had completely different life experiences but the fact that they were unwilling to jointly attend family gatherings unless it was absolutely necessary seemed petty and selfish. I would pick up on the tension on these occasions and oddly spend time engaging my dad's parents who, on the face of it at least, were the antagonists in this totally unnecessary ongoing family feud. I shouldn't have felt like I needed to give them my attention but somehow, I did.

I quickly learnt that telling jokes always went down well, as well as doing comedy voices ... it seemed to loosen them up and my grandad (Mum's dad, Leonard) especially responded with his own style of cheeky replies and we quickly formed a very close relationship that I thoroughly enjoyed right up to the age where it seemed kinda odd to still be hanging around with Grandad. He was a beautiful man who was so instrumental in my life in regard to learning about making stuff and tinkering with anything and everything. I've always had a restless inventiveness that I squarely contribute to Leonard, and my later career flip from the corporate world into the world of industrial design and furniture-making was as a direct result of what I learnt and witnessed by his side. He was very much like another father to me.

On the subject of Grandad, it's worth saying that I come from a very small family. Mum and Dad stayed married their whole lives, Mum was an only child, my dad had a brother who was childless. I have one older sister. Age-related guests at these functions – and, my oh my, were they functional – were non-existent.

Back to Grandad. My grandmother was an incredibly stubborn woman for reasons I couldn't fathom at a young age – she never worked a day in her life. Grandad had had a very well-paid job and took early retirement, so they had a wonderful standard of living and my mum being an only child meant there was none of the associated challenges of the competing demands that raising siblings can create. It is on this subject that I think Grandad and I bonded. I was the son he so desperately would have wanted. I'm not talking myself up here but I'm pretty sure any boy would have been amazing under his expert guidance. It's just he never got the opportunity to fulfil that potential of being a boy's father. I know Grandma found the experience of childbirth very unpleasant, though I don't believe there were any complications, and she decided that was that.

It wasn't long before I started actually enjoying the prospect of family get-togethers. I would make a mental note of various subjects, pay attention to the news to keep up to date on current affairs and committed things like jokes to memory over the preceding days and weeks. It gave me a sense of empowerment and control. Even today I find myself rehearsing a conversation I might have with somebody, so I'm well prepared when the moment arrives. This ended up having unwanted repercussions in my private life for example, when a conversation with my partner of the time didn't play out as I was expecting and I would react or get very frustrated. But on the flip side, this strategy paid dividends in my professional career in sales, as I was always well prepared for most scenarios. More on this later.

I saw it as a challenge to get a smile or get a conversation going with family members who seemed like they wished they were anywhere other than at the current family event. I may be wrong of course and deep down inside they could have been having a riot, but it certainly didn't feel or look like that. Looking back now these were my initial lessons into reading the room and feeling the energy.

As you get older (particularly if you are British), you will at some point get involved in banter. It's the grown-up equivalent of time wasting and filling the voids in what should really otherwise be quality conversation. It's a predominately male pursuit.

Banter is a strange process in which two or more people, very confident in their own ability to deliver witty quips, duke it out until essentially one person runs out of something funny to say. I became very good at this due to my ability of avoiding gaps in conversation at home and always having a few words loaded in the chamber, ready for that inevitable deathly silence.

It's like the vocab equivalent of a sword fight and it rarely ends with both combatants feeling they left on equal grounds. Invariably, it gets personal or if it doesn't get personal one person often goes too far and is just flat-out rude. The ability to always have the last word will ensure you always have a home on Costa del Banter and it was a place I called home very often.

Why did I include this at this point in the book? Well, it meant that I had basically created a 'gift of the gab' persona for myself which was to propel me into a sales career that would prove both lucrative and enjoyable for most of my professional life.

However, of course there is a downside. Banter is not always an equal dual, not everyone involved even signs up for it and it can be quite discriminating in terms of the barbs and darts that are thrown around during the so-called game. There can also be collateral damage. Indeed, in the early years of our relationship, Mel would call out my banter at times for what it was ... being a 'bit bitey'. And of course, the biggest downside, depending on how you look at it, is that it provides a mask for the real person to hide behind.

—— ❧ ——

CHAPTER 5

He Who Dares, Rodders, He Who Dares

Doves – There Goes the Fear (2002)

The inner confidence is starting to build and the world becomes one big game for me. I'm also reminded of the famous Del Boy line from Only Fools and Horses, *'He who dares, Rodders, he who dares', and I have named the chapter after it.*

LIKE ANY HOUSEHOLD in the 80s, Del and Rodney were comedy gold and a staple of evening viewing on the BBC.

I can safely say with a relative degree of certainty that, as I went through my later teenage years and far beyond, fear was not an emotion I possessed. I would dare myself to do things and make big decisions a lot and I developed a system to help me beat the odds. For me risk had rewards, and I was happy to take them on whilst somehow knowing deep inside it was going to be alright. 'I'll be alright' became my inner mantra.

It's kind of weird to write those previous sentences as I was a painfully shy child. I would blush at the merest hint of attention and if, during school assemblies where passages of the bible would be read, the name Philip (the Greek apostle) came up in the extract being spoken, I would blush uncontrollably. In fact if anyone came up to me and said, 'Hey, Phil, go red,' I would and it would take me quite a while to revert to normal skin colour.

I'm not exactly sure when I shed this skin but little by little my confidence grew as I started to take responsibility for my own decision making – if I'm honest, I never felt my parents had my best interests at heart and although that may sound callous and cold, I cannot easily recall either of them praising or supporting me unequivocally on anything ... or at least anything that mattered to me.

There was love there, I'm sure, but they just couldn't show it and to be fair they were just products of the time and their own circumstances and environment, having been born smack in the middle of WW2. I felt convinced it was my behaviour though that shaped their attitude towards me and no matter what I succeeded in or achieved – and, boy oh boy, did I try – their response or more accurately their lack of response was always the same.

However, even that belief was totally torpedoed one day in my early 40s during a trip back to the UK with a recently born Lyla and standing in my sister's kitchen. I'm not particularly close to my sister ... it's not that we don't get on and we've never had an argument from what I can remember, we just never had any positive experiences together as siblings that we relate to ... at least that's how I see it. Could be a boy girl thing? I am two years younger and was just into completely different things to her.

Anyway, just sipping on a cup of tea and nibbling on a custard cream, Maria says, 'Do you think Mum and Dad ever loved us?'

I was gobsmacked as that was exactly how I felt growing up and still do to be honest ... but I feel bad looking back now as I realise that was my sister's cry for help and I was so caught up in my own life (Lyla, my youngest, had epilepsy at the time) and having buried that time under so many layers of cement since, I gave it one of my go-to glib remarks and the conversation moved on ... probably to *EastEnders* or something.

I guess, in hindsight and with the benefit of 20/20 vision, that what she felt was love but not a type that in any way nurtured or that we were aligned to.

Whilst researching for my book I have been reading other authors' memoirs. Many of them have a section in the book where as a youngster they vividly recall the first time they were heavily influenced by one of those childhood delinquents that all children and especially boys seem to come across in their lives. This is my version of that event and what I can clearly remember is, I wasn't one of those!

As living proof that I felt like my parents didn't really understand me as an individual or what made me tick, they decided without properly consulting me (which frankly they never did for anything) to get me a place on a Rotary trip with other kids to a weekend camp. I'm not exactly sure what Rotary is. Like the freemasons but legal? I was maybe 12 or 13. It was organised by the guy who owned the hardware shop that Dad worked at.

I was dropped off at the meeting point and the assembled mass of boys all stood around with their bags and waiting for instructions. I had a large group of mates at school and in my neighbourhood. I had overcome my shyness, so large groups didn't intimidate me and I had no trouble getting involved and making conversation. I ended up in a dorm with two other lads who were about my age or a little older. I seem to remember they knew each other. No dramas, I had some pretty good street smarts and they seemed to take me in without hesitation.

Well, if I thought I had street smarts then nothing prepared for what was to follow the next day. In fact, we didn't even have to wait until the next day ... That evening, when the group leader went around and ordered lights out, the two lads in my dorm went berserk. Jumping out of bed, slamming the dorm room door, running up and down the corridor, banging the toilet door and generally carrying on like a couple of clowns. The leader came around and ordered them back to bed where they promptly told him to go fuck himself. I was blown away by how anyone could have such little respect for authority. I mean I wasn't the best-behaved kid in school or round our way, but I knew basic right from wrong and I knew this was wrong.

Eventually things calmed down and we all got some sleep. The next day it all kicked off again.

There was a tuck shop in the main building. I'd been given some money by my parents – not much as was always the case when getting handouts from them, but it was enough for a Mars bar and Coke or whatever.

Anyway, the lads from my dorm waited until the coast was clear and in one fully orchestrated movement vaulted the counter and started wrenching the doors open on the cabinets. They reached inside and started raking out great armfuls of whatever they got their hot and sweaties on, passing them around to the rest of us slack-jawed kids witnessing this carnage.

My risk-reward logic kicked in immediately and I got the hell out of there ... this was trouble with a capital T. When cornered by the lads later I told them that I'd gone to keep a look-out up the end of the corridor in case anyone should head their way. Since they hadn't got caught, my story was watertight.

My moral compass would be tested later again that afternoon but for now there was fun stuff like football and abseiling to be getting on with. I've always enjoyed most adventurous activities and have no fear of heights; I am a strong climber as well as being fleet of foot and quick with my hands. It was an enjoyable set of activities and I found a bunch of lads similar in physique to me and we all egged each other on to get the most out of it. Then it was back to my dorm buddies, or should I say Doomsday buddies, for the afternoon treasure hunt in the local town.

We were given instructions of where to go, places to visit and a scorecard to keep. It all seemed pretty straightforward and I took the lead role since I was convinced I might be the only one with any brains between us. I wouldn't have to wait long to be proved right.

So, picture the scene, we are in a quaint little English country-side village. The place is what you would call a small market town with the necessary high street, train station and numerous parades of shops. So, there I am looking at the map and working out our first point of call when the Doomsday brothers leg it off in the opposite direction and head up the steps to the local church. I was lost for words and couldn't believe I'd had them figured out all wrong. I naturally turned to follow, not because I was religious but because I knew we needed to stick together. I hadn't even gotten the bottom step when they both came marching out the church doors very purposefully and without raising any suspicion, carrying the donations box. It was mental: they went around the corner as if it was something they did every day and sat down to check out the spoils from their ill-gotten gains. They plucked a few fivers out first then tipped out the coins. I have no idea what my face looked like but they were very fair when they split the loot three ways and proceeded to just saunter off down the road leaving me with six pounds 45 pence and a trashed donations box. I'd never seen anything like it and I have never since ... I was in shock.

What was I supposed to do? What does my logic gate do with this amount of information? I knew I couldn't touch the box and get my fingerprints on it ... I couldn't trust that they wouldn't blame it all on me (no such thing as CCTV back then), so I couldn't get the rozzers involved and besides these kids were clearly right off The Estate and if you're from Brighton and you know these estates and their reputation, you cover your ass. I walked around for a while, a bit dazed and confused and clutching the money, thinking that if I was apprehended, I would fall off that bridge when I came to it. Nothing happened as I walked back to the campsite and on the final few metres, I popped into a newsagent and did the most bizarre thing – I bought the latest car mag. I guess my rationale was to absorb myself in it in the dorm and for the rest of the day as we were going home in the morning. I honestly cannot tell you what happened on my return, if I had conversation with the boys or not, one of whom incidentally looked like Ziggy from *Grange Hill*, if there is anyone reading who remembers that.

I was so traumatised I don't remember getting picked up, the ride home or even that evening. We were such a closed family that I certainly didn't speak about it and I certainly wasn't asked how it went so didn't feel the need to lie. I only shared that story with my parents a few years back and even then, there was still the minimum of reactions.

Did my dad even bother to ask who was going on this camp?

Either way, it furthered my resolve that my parents weren't serving my interests well and I continued to move in my own direction.

Meanwhile, as life returned to normal and I buried things under more cement, my confidence grew and grew like the proverbial snowball. I started to work out that it was me and me alone who was going to get me into and through life. I started to gather momentum, an arsenal of tools to get me through and also a radar for those who were with me or against me. I was not going to carry anyone. This would require more and more cement that only in recent years have I started to shed to reveal the true essence of me again – the sensitive boy and then man that I am.

I wasn't afraid of work, so I got a job with my uncle at his second-hand car lot in Brighton, which you will learn in the next chapter came with its own set of issues and quickly earned and learnt enough to forgo the little amount of assistance I was being provided with, which in the short term at least led to good outcomes for me, which then positively reinforced that what I was doing was working.

I developed my own logic gate system for decision making and very quickly became quite adept at working out all the possible permutations for which way a decision could go and then making an informed decision very quickly. Once that decision was made, I was so confident in my foolproof process of achieving it I would move heaven and earth to make it a reality. Terms like 'bull at a gate' and 'dog with a bone' could be interchangeable sayings. Once achieved, I became so fixated on the outcome, I couldn't understand why no one else was as invested in it as I was. This would then lead me to going it alone even more so.

Calculation became my modus operandi. That is, rather than being able to be present and in the flow of life which allows you to feel your way through, discern and respond, calculation means going into reaction, protection and drive. A whole chapter is coming up on this!

Looking back now, it is probably when my life became Phil vs The World. Fear and failure I thought would never feature in my life again … oh boy, how wrong you can be.

Also, at this time due to the extraordinary effort I was putting into rowing conversations along on the home front I would regularly be told I had 'the gift of the gab'. But let's face it, compared to the competition I was facing at these events it was hardly praise worth celebrating. However, I understood it was for the most part a compliment and since they were in short supply round my house, I saw the moniker as a badge of honour and happily wore it with pride.

It's a well-worn expression, though I've never fully looked at its origins, but it was a neat little saying that rolled off my increasingly silver tongue with ease.

CHAPTER 6

The Law of Supply & Demand

Pet Shop Boys – Opportunities (1986)

In this chapter I start to explore my skills as an astute school-age boy who is very dedicated to keeping his hobbies afloat. Another thing I learnt from reading other authors' memoirs is that they devote a section to when they suddenly became aware of their ability to trade up. Whether it be your remote-control car, your train set or any one of the numerous hobbies that any young boy would have.

AT SOME POINT in my early teenage years, I started to become aware of, shall we say, trading and the art of negotiation and how one can benefit from it financially.

As a kid I was always looking for new hobbies and from as far back as I can remember, I was finding out ways to fund them. Whether it was fishing, bikes, train sets, slot cars, music, hi-fi or any other hobby any self-respecting boy would be into.

I grew up in a fairly humble household where, whilst we had things like two cars and a large bedroom each for my sister and me, it always felt like money was tight and we almost always never ever spoke about it ... or the lack of it.

In the early years, hobbies would be funded by money from my parents and grandparents at Christmas or birthdays but as my tastes grew more exotic and expensive, I had to look at alternative methods. Swapping with mates, or should I say finding new mates who were into what I was now fixated by, became the norm and understanding the relative value of something was paramount. I'm pretty sure every time I undertook a barter or trade with my mate I would – at least from my point of view – come out on top in terms of now owning something that wouldn't be possible through other means available to me.

There was one event that sticks clearly in my mind that I learnt a good lesson from. I had to beg, borrow and steal (joint Christmas and birthday presents from all family members) to be the proud owner of an Atari 2600 games console. They were everywhere at the time and nothing flash, but they made you feel like a million dollars when you turned it on, slotted the cartridge in, got your vertical hold just right and started smashing your joystick – that's not a euphemism for something, though plenty of that wasn't too far away, mind.

The console came with a couple of games – Pac-Man and some bomber aeroplane game. I managed to fluke an extra game called something like Meteor Dash 1000 as it was on special when I got it from Comet. Our modest background meant finding the money for extra games was out of the question, so I devised another plan.

I desperately wanted Pole Position. It was a huge arcade game classic at the time and even the home console version was hugely entertaining. Being a total car tragic, it was the only thing I really wanted more than anything in the world.

At the bottom of my road there was a parade of shops and like most suburban parades of shops there was always a second-hand shop that had anything from furniture, golf clubs to prams and such like. They were the precursor to Cash Converters, I guess.

For about a week or so I asked a couple of my school mates to go into this shop and ask the bearded old dude in there if he had any Atari games for sale, which I knew he didn't as I had been in and had a look around. I told them to specifically ask for Pac-Man and Meteor 2000. They thought I was bonkers, of course – no one wanted these games as they came free with the console.

Then, after the bait had been cast, I went in and asked the guy if he wanted to buy any Atari games. He said, 'Yeah sure, what you got?'

I explained I had a few and made up a list of non-existent titles; he said no but he was looking for Pac-Man and Meteor 2000. I feigned surprise and said, 'Oh yeah, I might have those. I'll check and pop back.' Anyway, I sent my mate in one more time to keep him keen and he said he should have something the following week. Perfect ... I went in the next day and sold him both my games, which was thereabouts enough for Pole Position and neither me nor my mates ever went back in the shop. The games sat on the shelf for ages and I felt bad every time I walked past on my daily walk to and from school. I'm sure the bearded guy worked out the ruse as he would have seen me and my mates all hanging around together down at the parade, but nothing was ever said.

As a footnote to this story, later I got into radio-controlled cars in a big way – Tamiya was big back then and my Super Champ used enough batteries to sink a battleship. Some were rechargeable but the servo batteries weren't. They devoured AAs at an astounding rate of knots and this guy had some non-brand ones that seemed on the face of it at least good value compared to Duracell or Eveready. I went in to see what kind of deal he would do on a whole box and we promptly agreed on a price and I left clutching my own body weight in AAs. I couldn't have been happier. Now I don't know if he remembered me or I was just unlucky but over the next few months every time I needed to replace the batteries which was often, I would go to my stash and find they were either already dead or had leaked all their acid over the rest of the contents and ruined them too.

No bad deed goes unpunished would be an appropriate line for this experience. It did at least teach me one thing that I would take with me through life: be honest in business dealings.

CHAPTER 7

———— ⌬ ————

Becoming the Storyteller

BBC Jackanory theme tune (circa 1980)

This following story is included simply because it's an amazing story about the fragility of life and death but unlike the word 'jackanory', which is often used – in the UK at least – to describe a fictitious event, this is most definitely not one of them.

A quite simply mind-blowing event happened in July 1986 that would test my ability to think on my feet, talk and think fast – and run fast and stare down fear in order to save the life of not just myself but my uncle (Dad's half-brother) too.

FIRST SOME CONTEXT. My dad has a half-brother, Michael. Interestingly I didn't find out about this – about him being a half-brother that is, not that he existed, but that he was a half-brother – until I was randomly looking through our bureau at home one day. In it I found my dad's adoption papers from when my granny and grandpa adopted my dad from his biological dad ... my real Grandpa Sidney, if you will. It felt like I'd stumbled across our family's little secret and the one time I did bring it up, it took my dad so close to violence – he is a very placid man but I was well aware there was anger there if you scratch through the thin veneer of the British 'nothing to see here' – that I never brought it up again and it certainly was never spoken about willingly by my parents. I couldn't believe the deception. Looking back now, I realise all too clearly my dad was clearly damaged from his own father abandoning him and that he couldn't break the cycle and learn to show love to his own son. However, on a recent visit to Australia, he brought with him not only a photo of my biological grandfather but also a willingness to converse about the possibilities and probabilities of why he came to be adopted. Remember, my parents were born in the thick of WW2; a lot of men went away to war and didn't always come back home into the loving arms of the women they left – not through fault of their own or that of their wives but that sometimes it was not known if their husbands were coming home. All speculation of course, as he just did not know the answers.

Michael's personality, being Dad's half-brother, is not even close to Dad's personality. Back then, Michael was a fast-living and fast car-driving individual whose lifestyle for many years when I was a child was hugely captivating. He drank and smoked and was the complete antithesis of my dad and I feel terrible for saying it, but I put him (Michael) on a pedestal. My dad had his faults but please don't think this book is some kind of beat-up job on either of my parents. He was a hardworking and extremely practical man who just didn't seem very happy. Sure, he would smile and laugh but I always felt he was covering up many of his true emotions. We never sat and just chatted. Or did anything just the two of us.

If you haven't already guessed, I'm obsessed with cars ... always have been. It's in the blood ... on my dad's side we have a relative called George Noble who used to race at tracks like Brooklands in

Bugattis amongst other various machinery. And also, on my dad's side, whilst not strictly cars we do have a close relative who started the JAP motorcycle company which was a contemporary equivalent to BSA and Norton. Petrol is in the veins, so to speak.

My dad took no real interest in having a fast car whereas Michael raced go-karts and owned a Lotus, Ferrari and Sierra Cosworth to name but a few. He did, however, live at home with Granny and Grandpa until they died, and he never seemed to have a stable relationship. My dad, in contrast, married the girl next door, literally next door in the cul de sac they lived in growing up and would remain faithful his whole life, renovate multiple houses as the family grew, have two children and generally what you would say in the UK, grind it out.

In energetic terms, I had been taking donations from my uncle for many years and unfairly been comparing him favourably to my dad. I got the impression Michael's behaviour annoyed my dad intensely, but he was the favoured child of the two – perhaps down to the fact he was my grandpa's biological son whereas Dad was adopted from my granny's previous marriage. Subsequently he got away with a lot more.

Back to the story. Michael owned a second-hand car yard in Brighton at the top of a steep hill overlooking Brighton station. Always on the lookout for cheap labour, he suggested to my dad that I work at the garage on Saturdays to clean cars and run errands.

I was more than happy to accept, despite the meagre wages. I got a lift to and from work in some nice motors and was surrounded by cars that I worked on during the day. Tasks included small body repairs, generally spivying the cars up and getting them looking their best. This wasn't always so straightforward as they for the most part were old bangers. Occasionally a nice Jag, Rover or Mercedes would come through the yard and I would always make an extra effort to make these cars shine.

On the side, Michael bought what was one of the first Jet washing machines in Brighton. It was a beast of a thing that ran on some type of inflammable liquid (kerosene or paraffin, I seem to recall) and its engine and compressor and water pump ejected scalding hot water or steam at a ridiculous rate of knots.

The idea was that during English winters, which the whole world knows to be pretty severe, the salt from the icy roads caused untold damage to cars on the road that could be steam-cleaned and many owners were happy to pay for the privilege of having it done. Then there were all the trade clients who wanted a car they had in for resale to have the engine, wheel arches and body steam-cleaned, which it has to be said brought them up looking like brand new. That was clearly good for resale value.

Every Saturday and not just during winter, there was a long procession of cars snaking up and down the hill and at seven quid for a full wash it was lucrative work ... for my uncle. My six quid a day for standing in a large puddle of water, getting freezing cold and soaking wet, seemed like a slightly less lucrative use of time. Sometimes the owners of cars would take pity on me and tip me once they had given Michael the appropriate fee. It was gruelling work, but it gave me money to fund other things in my life. Drinking and girls were starting to feature quite heavily and let's just say I put my money to good use.

One of the worst parts of cleaning the cars was doing inside the front arches. Years of baked-on mud and grime needed to be hosed off and as I got to the back of the arch invariably a spray of scalding hot filthy water would eject directly into my face out of the gap between the top seam of the wing where it meets the windscreen pillar, leaving me soaking wet, dirty and generally pretty unsatisfied with my current employment. This would happen on average at least 10 times a day. On the days where Michael decided he wasn't going back to Granny and Grandpa's (where he lived and I would get a lift), the bus was my only choice to get home and I would make the 30-minute journey back. Wet from head to toe, dirty but at least six pounds better off. Which, unbelievably, at the time still seemed worth it.

One of the issues of steam cleaning a car's engine is that hot water vapour gets into the engine's electrical system, the distributor, coil and high-tension leads. Very often, especially with Fords, this meant the car refused to re-start on the car lot ... or, more accurately, the swamp of mud and oily water in which I stood.

The solution was somewhat inelegant in that I would push the car backwards out the yard and instruct the helpless owner who was by now wondering quite how he had ended up in the situation to point the car downhill and bump start it. Almost no cars in the UK were automatic back then so it was a viable option.

The instructions, to put it in top gear, keep the clutch depressed until the car was halfway down the hill then drop the clutch, were duly administered.

Sometimes I didn't have the heart to stand and watch the outcome in case the poor driver should get to the bottom of the hill, which was a busy junction, and still not be firing on any cylinders. They were now stranded in no man's land with no means of forward propulsion, but the hill was so long and steep that those owners couldn't be bothered to attempt the trek back up to either complain or get help.

Due to this quirk of Ford engines, a system was devised whereby someone (normally the owner) would sit in the car and keep the engine running at round 3–4k RPM whilst the engine was cleaned. This worked a treat – until one day it did not.

When I wasn't working, Michael soon found standing in a quagmire of filthy water was not all that it was cracked up to be and so would offer the owners the chance to wash the cars themselves for a discount on the fee.

This was mainly for trade clients as retail business generally happened on the Saturdays when I was working. Trade clients who were keen to save a quid here and there soon started arriving with two people in the car – one to wash and one to keep the engine running.

From the police report I've read, this particular day was like any other normal midweek day at the car yard. A car was getting cleaned with the engine running. Except this time the guy cleaning the car was giving the cylinder head a really good going over and got the metal lance of the jet wash up close to the spark plugs ... too close, it would turn out, for an engine getting thrashed about at around four thousand revs. The voltage from the spark plug leads arced across to the metal lance and due to the enormous amount of standing water on the floor the guy who stood there proceeded to electrocute himself to death, right there and then. Gruesome!

I'm not sure exactly what happened in the next hours, but the ambulance came and CPR was given, but he was pronounced dead.

Days of mayhem ensued with Michael frantically running around giving police statements and filling out reports.

It was the summer of 96 and I was in the middle of my General Certificate of Secondary Education, known as GCSEs (like the HSC in NSW, Australia), and on study leave.

School was very kind to me academically and I didn't have to work too hard to achieve good grades throughout my school life. I had no reason to think end-of-school exams would be any different so when Michael asked me to look after the garage whilst he was up to his ears in paperwork with the authorities and knowing there wasn't going to be any steam-cleaning for quite a while, I jumped at the chance to earn a bit extra.

Had I known what was coming, I would have asked for hazard pay.

I remember so clearly. It was one of those beautiful English summer days. I was just wearing my cutdown jeans and sitting in the yard on an old converted car seat that had been turned into a chair. I was drinking a can of Coke and this huge guy walked into the yard. I actually thought at the time, 'Jeez, you're a lump', but stood up and made my way over to him and asked him if he needed any help.

My job when Michael wasn't around just like any other day of the year was to talk to potential punters, give them prices of the cars and take details if there was any follow-up required.

He said he wanted to know how much the silver Chevette was, so I said, 'Sure come into the office and I'll take a look.'

We never had those illuminous figures you often see on windscreens in most second-hand car yards; instead, Michael wrote out an A4 piece of paper each week with prices for cars and his tick list for money owed from trade accounts for steam-cleans. This was left in the office for me to use for clients. When I tell this story I usually say that the office went dark as the frame of this hulk filled the open doorway. I'm not sure if that is necessarily true but it does paint the required picture.

There were a couple of desks in the small damp office with the prerequisite table for tea and coffee and a filing cabinet in the corner.

As I stood next to one of the desks looking for the price list, I could see this guy's eyes dart around the room and finally come to rest on the *Evening Argus*, the Brighton local rag. The newspaper, which was folded in half, was showing the front page and it read something like 'Man dies in local carwash'.

It was certainly a confronting image especially if, as it turned out in the case of this guy, you were his brother.

He took no time in telling me, 'You killed my brother now I'm going to kill you!'

And with that he swung a huge clenched fist in the direction of the side of my face, which I saw coming (how could I not, it was like a wrecking ball coming towards me). Being quite fast and with good reactions I did my best to avoid it, but it still landed hard on my neck and with me being the lithe eight-stone teenager I was, it had the effect of sending me flying across the office, where I ended up in a heap between the filing cabinet and tea/coffee table.

As I came to – I was pretty sure I was unconscious for a brief moment – he picked me up with one hand around my chin and was now pointing a 6-inch hunting knife at my throat. A hunting knife is a sheath knife but with that serrated part on the back, usually used for cutting branches when building a shelter and not for some teenager's throat.

Time to think and fast … I tried to reassure him that no one had killed his brother, it was just a terrible accident involving a cleaning machine.

It was difficult to talk as my throat had swollen from the punch and quite frankly, I was bricking myself.

I do think that at that stage he had a moment of self-realisation and considered his options as he relaxed his grip and took a step or two back from me.

I'm not sure of the exact next dialogue but he knew Michael owned the place and asked where he was. Luckily, he was out … well, not luckily for me but lucky for him at least.

In those days a lot of car traders (and stockbrokers, if you believe the adverts) had those big brick-like mobile phones. He told me to call him and get him up here as he was going to kill him.

So, what were my choices really? I couldn't summon Michael to what seemed like a certain death sentence and watch him get attacked in front of me. So I picked up the phone and started dialling. As mobile phones weren't all that common back then there weren't many differences in digits between people's numbers. Especially if they were from the same area. I knew a mate of Michael's had a similar number (maybe a digit or two different), so I rang that instead. I had no idea if he was watching me dial or knew what Michael's number was. It was a push-button trim phone, so unless you were some kind of secret agent trained in the art of surveillance, there was no real way of deciphering which buttons had been pressed if you did it quick enough.

Michael's mate answered and I said, 'Hey Michael, it's Phil here. Can you get up to the garage straight away please?'

Obviously, his mate was confused and corrected me by saying, 'It's not Michael, Phil. Wrong number.'

'Yeah, I know,' I said, and repeated the request for him to get to the garage.

I had the phone pressed so hard to my ear it was hurting, along with my neck and throat.

'Is everything okay, Phil?' came his mate's reply.

'Yeah, look, I'd just really appreciate if you could get up here right away as there's someone here to see you.' I offered and put the phone down before I was properly busted.

Then another strange thing happened. Some official-looking guy with a clipboard wandered into the car yard and approached the office. The door was open and he looked in to see what I imagine would have been a guy with a hunting knife still held aloft and a school kid in nothing but cutdown jeans and trainers looking very disorientated.

The feeling I had was like the one I imagine people who have been on a deserted island for years and see an aeroplane flying low overhead have.

Old mate swung around to face the door and pointed the knife in the direction of Mr Clipboard – who promptly headed off the way he'd come in.

I was gutted ... just like the person on the deserted island, who despite lighting the fire and scrawling a message in the sand, watches as the aeroplane continues on its path and disappears out of sight and over the horizon.

The big guy then asked what happened on the day his brother died. I suspected he already knew the answer, but I wasn't about to let the question go unanswered. I said that he had been using the steam-cleaning machine and got electrocuted. 'I want to see the machine,' came his reply.

Due to the area the garage was located in, break-ins were regular and because it was an expensive piece of machinery Michael had built a brick cupboard with multiple locks and padlocks.

The keys were hanging where they were always to be found, on the board with all the keys for the cars in the yard.

I grabbed them as I walked to the workshop. I did consider briefly making a dash for it as the entrance to the yard was right in front of me, but fear had taken over. Obviously, comparisons are made to thriller movies at this point, when you're yelling at the main character on the screen, 'Just run! What the hell is the matter with you?' Well, for me it was simply realising that the big guy following me had quite a long reach: I was fearful he would grab me and as he was still holding the knife it wasn't a risk worth taking, even though I knew I was quick out the blocks and had good wheels myself. As I walked to the less than professional-looking brick cupboard,

I was thinking if I could just buy myself time, there would be more options. I wrestled with the padlocks and slide bolts and swung the door open. Again, when I tell the story I make a point of describing the creaking sound the door made (which it did) in an eerie way and there, covered in tons of grease and grime from many years of hard use was the machine in question. Really, all it needed was the big guy's brother's trainers still smouldering in there to make the scene complete; thankfully, that was not the case.

Even so it was still enough to send him into a fit of rage and then, for the second time in too short a time, he proceeded to belt me round the head. This time square on the jaw, which sent me sprawling back onto the workshop floor and sliding under a car that was up on axle stands. As I lay there looking up at the greasy underside of some old banger, I considered playing dead or being unconscious. You know how you see in the movies, to put the assailant off the scent?

But survival and no-fear mode kicked in eventually and I scrambled to my feet knowing I just had to get the hell outta there. Even for a talkative young chap like me, I was done talking to this guy.

I emerged battered and bruised from the workshop with one thing on my mind and that was to get the funk out of Dodge.

However, that wasn't quite as straightforward as I'd imagined it would be, as there were probably half a dozen or so dog squad in the entrance with animals straining at the leads and guys dressed in full combat attire. One with a handheld tannoy. To say I was shocked was to put it lightly. I turned to see where big guy/knife man was and as I did I saw along a perimeter wall of the car yard another half a dozen or so policemen in full riot gear – I couldn't tell you whether they had guns or not – encircling the yard.

By now big guy/knife man was out the workshop too and decided to divert his attention to the police, yelling things like, 'They killed my brother!' as well as other expletive-laden tirades. The guy with the tannoy beckoned me to approach him as my assailant was preoccupied with a policeman, who was now talking to him like a hostage negotiator. He mouthed and gesticulated that it was safe to make a run for it. Well, let's just say I didn't need any more encouragement. I took off like a greyhound chasing a hare, got through the gates, ran up the hill and just kept running. A funny comment from an ex-girlfriend who I was telling this story to said, 'What, just like Forrest Gump?' If you've watched the movie, you'll know the 'Run, Forrest, run!' scene.

As I bolted up the hill, I side-stepped two policemen with consummate ease as adrenaline coursed through my veins and the three of us then continued to run up to the top of the hill and down the other side. The T-junction at the bottom had by now been cordoned off and there were a few stationary police cars with lights flashing.

I came sprinting down the hill and a few policemen readied themselves and blocked my progress; I was willingly herded into one of the already opened police cars, at which point the doors were closed, sirens and lights went on and we sped away across town to Brighton police station. I don't remember much of the next few hours, but I was processed as a victim of a crime and a witness statement was taken – and of course, I drank lots of tea. Though that wasn't easy as my throat had all but swollen up. As I was under 18, my parents had to be informed and the police set about tracking them down.

My dad's half day from the hardware store where he worked was on a Thursday and as was always the case he could be found in the garden. The police did not know that, however, so when they rang the house there was no answer. A couple of uniformed coppers were then sent round. They went around the back and found my dad. I wasn't the most law-abiding kid growing up: nothing serious like breaking and entering or violence, just knocking about on the streets late at night with my mates, which would sometime result in a lift home in the back of a police car ... which we all thought was marvellous, of course.

My dad no doubt thought I was up to no good when he saw the uniformed police marching through the back gate.

The situation was fully explained and after about an hour or so my dad arrived to take me home.

The journey home was the most surreal experience. There was no talking (just as well really, as my windpipe had all but totally contracted) and we both sat in the front in stunned silence. There were no big hugs or displays of any affection. Just a functional exchange between two people who had known each other for seventeen years.

Meanwhile, back at the car yard, apparently big guy decided he wasn't yet done for and tried to ramraid his way out the yard. He re-entered the office, grabbed a handful of keys from the board and headed back out. Then, as was always the case with Hilltop Motors, the car wouldn't start, which put paid to his plans. So, as I'm led to believe, he jumped out the car and climbed up on the roof of the workshop to make an escape through the surrounding gardens but – again in true comedy-caper script fashion – the roof gave way under his huge frame and the police swooped in and apprehended him.

It turns out the guy with the clipboard was a health and safety inspector who had been sent to do a full assessment on the operation safety of the garage following the death. He managed to flag down a passing police car that just happened to be in the vicinity and raised the alarm. What a report he was going to be writing!

I never did find out what happened to Michael's mate I called.

Back at chez Hillsy later that afternoon, after Mum had also come home and I'd consumed my own body weight in tea and biscuits, there was the familiar sound of a loud exhaust and revving engine, which could only mean the arrival of one person.

Dad answered the doorbell and after a few of seconds of chitter chatter he announced Michael was here, which I assumed meant I was to get up off the couch and go and see him.

What followed by far and away was the most depressing part of this entire sorry story.

There was some brief 'Hey Phil, how you going?' kind of stuff and then the subject quickly turned to money and he said something like, 'I suppose I should pay you for today?'

He then proceeded to pull out his wad of cash from the back pocket of his jeans.

Like most people who deal in a lot of cash he had no room for it all in a wallet so he kept it in his back pocket in rolled-up fashion, with the largest denominations on the outer decreasing towards the centre.

Fifties are the largest note in the UK and Michael always had plenty of those. The wad was pulled out and I thought at the very least getting a 50 or a couple of them was appropriate given the circumstances. I shouldn't have got ahead of myself as we were quickly into the 20-pound notes. But no, deeper we went into the wad ... finally, a couple of tens were extracted from the bulging mass of money. I think at that point my daily rate was 10 pounds, so it amounted to nothing more than double pay. Or Sunday pay. I couldn't believe it, but I probably should have, to be honest, as it was classic Michael. I expected Dad to say something like 'Is that all my son's life is worth?' but it never came of course and no sooner had Michael arrived, he left. Without even so much of a right rollicking from my dad, which I would have really appreciated.

I recovered well and as the next day was Friday – which meant pub night – I went down there, cashed up or relatively so, and was met with cheers from my mates as they had heard what had happened on the TV. Plus the girls were falling over themselves to give me attention, so all in all the whole event seemed to have some positives. However, the part that benefited me the most – at least I thought it did until I realised that it had allowed me to develop a mask to hide the true me behind for a lot of my life – is that it signalled the beginning of Phil the Storyteller.

A few years ago, I retold the story to Mum and Dad over dinner when they were on a trip to Australia. They obviously knew about it but given the type of family we were I don't think we'd ever actually spoken about the details and to my absolute amazement there was no emotion or input from them only to defend my uncle whom I was still obviously dirty with. After all these years they seemingly still failed to grasp the severity of the whole incident and its effect on their seventeen-year-old son.

I've told that story umpteen times but writing it down has caused me to shed a few tears – it was huge. I didn't realise how big a hurt I had been carrying around all these years. Again, I don't blame my parents. It is how they were brought up and parented. We can harden from our hurts and this can stop us from acting or expressing who we truly are. I know this happened to me and many around me.

PART THREE

GOING IT ALONE. GETTING A CAREER. FINDING COMFORT IN MONEY.

When I felt like it was up to me to make my way in the world. A very basic binary attitude was developed: you were with me or against me – no shades of grey.

CHAPTER 8

The Great Escape

Pink Floyd – Another Brick in the Wall (1979)

This is another huge moment that would fall into the 'Feather Duster, Brick and Bus' analogy. This was most definitely a brick, as I was fortunate enough to be spared the bus on this occasion – much to my continued amazement!

I T ALL STARTED perfectly innocently enough. Standard operating procedure around the time of my early 20s was to work hard Monday to Friday at my American Express job, then get up to all kinds of nonsense and go on a proper roar-up at the weekends. For the purposes of setting the scene for this story, the weekends would start at any time from Friday lunchtime, with what most people would call 'drinking your lunch' or having a 'wet lunch', and end at an unpredetermined time at least 48 hours later. To save you doing the maths quickly, it often wouldn't end before Sunday lunch and sometimes later still.

The start time was more or less exactly 12.10pm, which was 10 minutes after the official lunch hour began plus the 10 minutes it took to get clear of building, walk the short distance to the pub, head to the bar and order your drink, which would invariably be a pint of strong European lager. Kronenbourg if it was on tap was the preference; Löwenbräu and Warsteiner were de rigueur and couldn't be overlooked either, but trusty old Stella was also more than acceptable. Low-strength brands like Carling or Fosters or Carlsberg were very frowned upon for anyone seriously considering a decent career in pub drinking which, let's face it, was the side hustle that the majority of 20-year-olds applied themselves in. At least it was where I grew up and I'm fairly certain it was all over the UK in the late 80s. Food wasn't imperative: eating wasn't looked down upon exactly, but the general consensus was that breakfast, lunch or dinner were for a beginner. You know the saying: Eating is cheating! What a way to think, but think that we did.

Looking back, it's amazing how this was always conducted, orchestrated and executed like a military manoeuvre with ruthless efficiency. But what happened after the first 12 hours was anything but clinical. We would head to the nightclub around 11pm after multiple other drinking establishments had been visited, then we'd sometimes go on to another nightclub open later, say the Ministry of Sound up in London. Someone would be driving, so we would head off around 3am and get back for 6 or 7am as it was only an hour's or so trip from Brighton. We would go back to someone's flat for more drinking and smoking and it would end sometime around Sunday or Monday. All this would be achieved with no sleep.

So, to the brick incident. My memory is very hazy, but at some point, after one of these long weekends, I left my girlfriend's flat in Brighton to head to my parents as I needed to get changed and grab a bag of clothes for the week ahead. I hadn't officially moved into my girlfriend's place by this point, so I was for all intents and purposes still living at home, about six miles away. Most if not all my belongings were still there. At about 8pm I jumped into my car, which at the time was an Alfa Romeo Sprint, and headed off. This is where it gets interesting. It was not a big drive and one I had done countless hundreds of other times as it was a well-worn route for commuters between a lot of the South Coast towns. The road was called the A259 and had mainly straight sections with a few traffic lights to navigate. I remember at about the halfway point I sat at some traffic lights and a wave of tiredness hit me. There weren't many other cars on the road to keep me focused. I set off for the last three miles of journey to the safety of my parents' home. Except I didn't get there safely. What followed was an unforgettable two hours of the greatest escape manoeuvres ever to play out. This is not fiction, I can assure you.

First thing I did was open the windows and sunroof and turn the music up loud. This was to keep me awake, not make me look cool! I most definitely did not look cool with what was about to unfold another mile or so down the road, although I did handle it pretty cooly if I'm being just a little bit modest for a sec.

It's a road I know very well, and I can definitely not remember leaving the traffic lights but about a minute or so later I awoke to the most enormous crashing sound. I had never been in a decent-size car accident before, but you don't need to have been in one to know what it sounds and feels like and this was one for sure. As I woke it took me a few seconds to regain my focus. I blinked and blinked to clear my eyes from sleepiness, but I still couldn't see clearly out the front windscreen. The car was stationary, of that much I was clear on. As I focused my vision still further now I was fully awake, I realised the windscreen was shattered. I had no idea where I was or what had happened so I pulled on the door handle and went to open it, but the door was jammed shut and no amount of shoulder barging would budge it. I scrambled over to the passenger seat and got myself free of the car. Still dazed and confused I looked back at the car, only to discover it had come to rest, embedded in a business's perimeter wall. I surveyed the scene, and my brain went into warp factor overdrive. Was I injured? Was I still drunk? Was anyone else involved?

After a brief survey of the scene, it was clear that this is what the police would call a 'single vehicle accident'. The area was deserted around this time of 8pm on a Monday night and it was clear I needed to get the hell outta there and pronto for the reason I'm about to explain in great detail, but it's worth the read. First, I'll say I'm going to jump around a bit in the story here; however, it's worth explaining that I had also around this time started to get sucked into the vortex of the underbelly of the Brighton scene. It was never more than a misstep away but finally the allure of not working the nine-to-five grind but inhabiting the party scene and all its riches full-time proved too great. Consequently, I found myself joining the nefarious group of illegitimate businessmen who make up a not insignificant part of the Brighton party culture. You have to remember that at this time the rave generation was getting well established all over the UK, and Brighton was very much at the epicentre of this cultural explosion. Not to put too fine a point on it, I became a small-time drug dealer to my close friends (nothing heavy, just pills and whizz) in a big pool of other players. Big revelation, I know, so let's take an even closer look at things to understand how it became so.

We have to go back to my first time at Amex, which spanned a few years. I had set myself the goal of becoming an airline pilot. Yeah, don't ask how I came to settle on this particular career choice, but I've always been interested in aviation and this sounded like an amazing thing to do. I had a weekend job at Shoreham Airport, a small municipal airport in the town where I grew up. My best mate's mum worked there at a place called Jade Engineering and they serviced and maintained small aircraft and helicopters. This benign Saturday job would further ignite my interest in aviation that would see me come up with ingenious ways to fulfil my dream.

I applied for a clerical duties job at Amex after I got back from doing a summer season on the Balearic Islands, mainly Magaluf, with my best mate at the time, Sam. There's a whole chapter in that time alone but I'll leave it well alone for the purpose of continuity. His mum, Sue, who got me the job at Jade Engineering, had moved to Magaluf and she invited Sam and me to go and stay there for the summer. I did pretty okay in my exams, so was more than employable for Amex office work. During the interview the lady asked what exactly it was I wanted to do at Amex. I wasted no time in telling her I wanted the best paying job possible. She looked through the vacancy list and asked if I would mind doing shift work at all. I've always been more of an owl than a lark, so the evening shift in the data collection department seemed ideal. I think I started later that week. I was now what was eloquently known as 'a tape monkey', which it was called colloquially. The work was okay. Basically, I had to load a round reel about 30cm in diameter onto a reel-to-reel data capture machine. This type of machine was very cutting edge back in the 80s and the Amex data room had banks and banks of these machines. If any of you have ever watched the original *Italian Job*, these are the machines used to provide the data for the city's traffic light system. In the movie, Michael Caine and others manage to swap a reel for another one programmed to cause absolute chaos in the Italian city they were in, by changing the phasing of the lights. Anyway, it was simple work, paid well because of shift loading and, due to the fact they contained vast amounts of card data, the machines would be in use 24 hours a day, which in turn meant extra overtime if one of the other guys on either the daytime or night shift failed to show. Which they often did. I've never been the sort of guy who's afraid of hard graft so I would pick up the extra shifts here and there. All this resulted in a decent weekly wage and I realised I could put a fair amount away each week after paying rent to my parents, putting petrol in the car and having a good Saturday night out. The shift work included a Friday night so I saved money not going out then. Very soon I had saved up the target amount of 5000 pounds, which was enough to begin my piloting dream. The way it worked was that you could go to the US and get your PPL (Private Pilot Licence). Then, after enough hours flying, you could convert it to a commercial licence, mostly by working on farms doing crop-spraying and the like. You would then move to doing flight tours for a commercial outfit and gradually get into bigger and bigger planes until you had enough experience to fly decent charter flights and would be an aircraft pilot in my definition of what one was. It was a tried and tested route and there were loads of companies offering a one-stop shop for this very career path. I was all fired up and ready to book my place on a course, but a strange feeling washed over me. That feeling was one of having money. What does money give me? If you've been paying attention, you'll know that from my upbringing where money wasn't in good supply, money was security and I wasn't going to let that warm blanket of financial freedom be taken off me in a hurry. This was despite even the prospect of a potentially rewarding career if I went and spent the money now. I just felt good in the knowledge it was there even if I now had no immediate plans for it. I continued to add to my stash over the months and maybe even the year.

I do remember one event where a financial advisor, who was the friend of a friend, was down at the pub we all drank at one night and telling a bunch of my mates how important it was to put away a little of your wages each week and watch it grow. The guy looked at me and asked if was working and if I was also putting a bit aside each pay check. I replied, 'Yeah sure, about a 100 pounds.' He said that's a great amount to do each month. I said, 'Each month? I'm doing that each week.' He nearly spat his mouthful of lager all over me. I was on a good wicket.

My partying continued and at a fairly respectable level, but the vortex of Brighton's inner pulse was beginning to strengthen and after meeting a new group of friends through the Amex social club, I got to experience the quality of the drugs on offer and life changed from this point forward. My hometown of Shoreham was a world away from this new life I had just experienced and a realisation dawned on me.

There was a lot of drugs being bought by this group of Brighton friends over the course of the weekend and it seemed to me they were paying way too much by not coordinating their purchasing power. At this time most of these friends were living pay check to pay check, so the notion of having enough money to bankroll their weekend activities in advance was somewhat limited. That's where I came in. I always fancied myself as a bit of a businessman and here now was the perfect opportunity.

The next time one of them went to buy the weekend's stash I asked him if I could tag along and meet the guy. I'm not sure if it's written down anywhere what the rules of engagement are for doing drug deals. I certainly hadn't been to a secret clubhouse where stuck to the back of the door was a dagger pinning an ancient scroll of papyrus outlining what to do and not to do. Upon meeting the guy who was not what I expected a typical dealer to look like – no shaved head, tattoos on his neck and knuckles, in fact he was just like me or any of my other mates – I asked him if we were to buy the whole lot in one go on a Friday, not on tick (i.e. paying at a later date, which was common practice) but by paying upfront, would the cost of each unit come down. He said yeah sure and we began talking specifics.

I very quickly after just a few minutes of chatting realised we had been paying way too much for not being organised in advance. We spoke about how it would work, ready for next Friday's pick-up.

The next Friday quickly arrived and our pre-arranged rendezvous was still on. I told all the Brighton crew what I was planning and there seemed to be nods of approval from all involved. There was a group of about 10 of us, all told. I asked them what they would need for the weekend and did a quick mental tally up. I met up with my guy as arranged and asked for the required amount which he had on him and more to spare so I bought a few extra. I had already got the cash ready, so we did the deal and he said if I ever needed any more that was no problem. I took the bag of goodies back to the guys and girls and handed them out, which they all eagerly took from me like kids taking sweets from a party organiser – which I suppose wasn't far from the truth. The weekend went as planned, but instead of having to scout around the club for the dealer who was serving up as the night wore on (every club has one), my friends were able to take advantage of the extras that I had bought earlier. So, I guess at that moment you could say I had made the first few tentative steps into drug dealing. You remember the guy asking me if I ever needed more, it was no problem? This stuck with me and I took it quite beyond what I think even he imagined.

So, with this in mind let's get back to where we left the story: me, surveying the scene immediately after the car crash ... and more than well aware of the large stash under the front seat. Not a good look if the police arrived. Writing this after all these years, there is more than a tinge of embarrassment at what occurred that night. I grabbed my stash and the bag with all my stuff in it and had the presence of mind to nick my own stereo, kicking the steering column about a bit to make it look like the car had been stolen. Checking the coast was clear, I headed out the way my car had entered the premises. Through the wall. I ducked in and out of gardens hidden by the shadows, keeping an ear out for the sound of police sirens, but they never came. Once I was well clear of the crash site, I found a pub and called my girlfriend who was just chilling out at home and told her to meet me at a certain place in 20 minutes. She was obviously pretty shocked to hear what I was explaining to her but she was very decent and drove to pick me up without fuss and we rode the short distance of three miles or so back home. When we got back about 9.30pm, I chatted with her flatmates about what had happened (they were all small-time drug dealers, like me – we all were!) and they also agreed to back the story that I had been home all night.

Remember there was no CCTV or traffic cameras around in those days. As you can probably imagine, I was pretty psyched up by the time I went to bed an hour or so later. I took a sleeping pill. That was probably the first one in my life ever as I consider myself an Olympic medal-winning sleeper. I was woken by the phone ringing and my girlfriend going to answer it. It was about 7.30am. My girlfriend had a bit of small talk with my dad who was on the other end. I couldn't really hear what was said but I was handed the phone and my dad explained that the police had rung him just now to say my car had been found on the property of a business by the caretaker of that company who was first to arrive at work that morning. He asked if I was OK, to which I replied, 'Yeah of course, why?' He then went on to tell me what the police had told him. He asked where my car was and I said, 'Out the front of the flat where I left it last night.' He said, 'No, I don't think it is, I reckon it has been stolen.' At this moment I put the phone down, walked over to the front window of the flat and actually looked out to see if I could see it, which I couldn't obviously and then walked back to the phone. I swore, which by the way I never did in front of my parents. I said the last time I saw it was when I parked it up last night. We chatted a bit more and Dad explained that because the car was registered at my parents' house in Shoreham, it was Shoreham police that wanted to see me.

He gave me the name of a policeman at the station and told me I should go down and see him. For some reason I've always been a two-car guy, so later that morning I jumped in my Triumph Spitfire and headed over to Shoreham, which was about a 20-minute drive away. I boldly strode into the police station and told the front desk officer who I was here to see. He asked me to take a seat as he would be with me shortly. I hadn't been in many police stations before and I can assure you they aren't very welcoming places. The policeman duly appeared and asked me to accompany him into an office. We both sat there in the room and the first thing he said to me was, 'Right, Phil, tell me what happened last night.' I proceeded to go through the version of events I had told my dad. He looked me up and down and I was totally unsure what he made of it all until he said, 'Righteo, OK then, can you roll up your sleeves and trouser legs, please?'

To which I duly obliged, not thinking what may be lurking under there. Without connecting the dots I said, 'Why? That's a strange thing to ask.' He replied, 'Well, because what normally happens in these situations is the owner has driven home drunk and crashed their car and then claims it was stolen.' There was a moment's silence and then he went on to say, 'But I can see you have no injuries and as far as we are concerned, whoever was in your car is injured so we've rung around all the hospitals and there has not been anyone presenting themselves.' I asked how bad was my car then, and he said it was in a pretty bad way. I feigned a shocked response and he said he would keep me updated if anything came of their investigations. I thanked him for his time and made a hasty retreat, not sure how to make any sense of it. I knew where the accident had happened so drove that way on my way back to my girlfriend's. It chilled me to the bone that on that stretch where I had left the road, there were buildings on one side and on the other were the docks and Shoreham harbour – along with gas storage tanks. How by some miracle the car decided to veer right instead of left into the harbour as I nodded off at the wheel was a ridiculous bit of luck. I had crossed the oncoming lane of traffic to end up in the wall, all of it unseen by anyone else – a great escape indeed!

There is a footnote to this story that is worth telling. At the time, my sister worked for an insurance company that my car was insured with and she was able to get me a favourable payout on the write-off. I knew where the salvage yard was that had the wreck, so I went down there to see the car. The policeman was right: it was in a pretty bad way but luckily I was not, especially considering I wasn't even wearing a seatbelt. Maybe the fact I was so loose and floppy saved me from serious injury, who knows? As I've said, a great escape if ever there was one.

If the brick analogy holds true, then what was the lesson to be learnt from this momentum-stopping event?

I've been talking about my car crash, but also about me becoming a pilot. Well, no surprises to learn that I didn't become a pilot. At the time I considered that I'd found a much better use for my money.

That last line provides a perfect segue to the lesson that was on offer here. If this turn of events wasn't serious enough to shake me from my stupor, something else happened afterwards that made me change lanes with my life. An event that I don't need to spend time going through now, but one that made me go legit. This event was about money and nearly losing it all. It's funny you know, I had it all. Money, popularity, no need to work but it ended up being the thought of losing my money that was the turning point. We as a race of humans often prioritise money over our safety, health and wellbeing. Why is that?

A saying that I have come to learn recently is that we use the first half of our life spending our health to build our wealth and the second half of our life spending our wealth to fix our health. Go figure, literally! Money is often cited as a measure of what it is to have a good life, to be successful in life. Positive psychology research conducted over many countries shows that there is a certain level of money that correlates to a good level of happiness or contentment. Having much more doesn't. Is it purely security then? Certainly, for me it has been about this for a lot of my life. Where did this come from? Why didn't I feel secure?

CHAPTER 9

When I Slammed into Drive

U2 – All Because of You (2005)

In this chapter I describe how I took my taste and hunger for sales to the next level! It was perfect – after all those years of yearning for adoration and recognition that I felt were missing growing up, I now had these in spades. Well, not always adoration. And was it enough?

ANY SALES GURU or sales course worth its fee will tell you that pauses or silence are a magical part of the sales process. And largely it's true.

It's the chance for the salesperson to gauge the appetite of their client after letting the proposal sink in and ask any questions or objections that can be handled accordingly. That's the theory anyway. I found doing things another way a bit more effective.

I had a few jobs in my late teens and early 20s that showed promise (a bit too much promise, as revealed in the last chapter) and could have led to a career. One such was as a turf accountant – a fancy name for a betting shop manager. Ladbrokes, in this case. I was training as a manager and had to be allocated to other shops from time to time. Brighton is surrounded by notoriously rough estates and on getting to work one morning I found the front door of one of our betting shops caved in, all the screens smashed to bits by baseball bats and the whole place rifled through by someone looking for easy money. Understandably, I left soon after that. But, as with most cases of life in Brighton, all roads eventually lead to American Express. And in my case I went back to Amex after my gap year of veering off course.

They had their European HQ on Edward Street in a fabulous white building, known colloquially as the 'wedding cake' due to its white tiered silhouette.

It was simply an awesome place to work, with so many people from the surrounding towns working there. You got a decent salary; the work was okay and the social life was out of this world, as previously described. Over the years I had a few jobs there, not least being the 'tape monkey' in its various forms, including senior tape monkey, but it was the last job I had there that really put a rocket under my career in the most unanticipated way.

As a bunch of lads socialising together in and around the pubs and clubs of BN1 (Brighton centre's postcode), we gradually one by one found work in this one department – Service Establishment New Accounts. It was simple data-entry clerical work but if your data was clean and fast there were good hourly pay rates on offer.

I've always had a healthy obsession with financial crime. I love a good story (has to be non-fiction) of someone who has got caught up in the messy side of finance and come unstuck, so when I was offered a position in the team (that team actually being just me) that performed credit checks on applicants to have Amex cards accepted at their establishment, I wasted no time in accepting. This credit checking was necessary, otherwise someone could set themselves up as a merchant accepting Amex cards and then stolen cards could be used to make fraudulent transactions where the merchant would get paid in exchange for no goods or services; the card holder would then dispute the claim in a genuine way and Amex would be left footing the bill.

It was great for a while but, inevitably, the larrikin style of me and all my mates caught up with us.

I seem to remember that there was a departmental party at the boss's house ... already sounds like trouble brewing, doesn't it? Things got a little loose. We were all big drinkers amongst other things and knew how to have fun. For some of the older managers, our particular style of fun seemed quite intoxicating, whilst others – our manager, in particular – found it disgusting. The house party started off benign enough, but the social lubricant was soon flowing and drinking games and dancing quickly gathered pace. I was single at the time and whilst not wanting to be in a relationship, I certainly wasn't backwards at coming forwards when the mood took me.

I do remember there was this older female manager from another department on the same floor who was getting quite wild on the dance floor, as indeed we all were. One thing led to another and I suddenly found myself in a bit of a clinch with her, which I really hadn't anticipated, and her language became rather unexpected. I don't need to go into what was said but suffice to say I went from Phil the brightly coloured chameleon to the camouflage-mode chameleon and looked to exit ASAP.

Back at work on Monday, everyone was talking about the party. Someone had spilled alcohol in the Koi carp pond and our boss wasn't happy, which was understandable, as some of her expensive fish died from alcohol poisoning. It was not confirmed as no autopsies were carried out but it seemed the most likely cause of death considering what went on. However, what surprised me in particular was that she was annoyed with me about the episode with this other manager. It had nothing to do with my manager whatsoever. What had I done wrong? I thought I'd behaved impeccably. And I was quite capable of not behaving impeccably, so I knew the difference very clearly. The gobby comments and snide remarks from her continued for a week until she really started to single me out for treatment. It came to a head one day over something or another, so despite the fact that I loved my job and was doing well at it, I decided using my tried and tested Phil logic gate system that my job was no longer serving me. I've always had issues with not being appreciated and this was one such occasion.

I went into town that lunchtime and visited a few recruitment agencies with the view to moving on workwise. I went into one agency, sat down and got chatting to the girl behind the counter. I told her I'd seen the sandwich board out the front with the sales roles that paid 13,000 pounds OTE (on target earnings). This was twice what I was on if I recall correctly and after what seemed a very brief conversation she said, 'You sound perfect. I'll get you an interview straight away.'

For some reason I've never been nervous around interviews. I find them a great opportunity to talk about the things that motivate me and my life's experiences that could benefit the company if I was in the role they were looking to fill.

I got offered the job in a very short time and handed in my notice immediately, much to the chagrin of my boss and co-workers.

My new job was to be at Nynex, a cable TV and telephone company, which was a very new thing at the time and as such was a world away from the corporate world of Amex. It was located in Fishersgate, a pretty down-at-heel satellite town outside Brighton, but what it did have going for it was parking on site. Parking had been a constant nightmare at Amex – even my prized Alfa Romeo got broken into one day and some little scrote robbed the stereo (the most important part at that age!), including the cassette that was in it. *Levelling the Land* by the Levellers, if I recall correctly.

Anyway, my new place of work was a windowless internal room in which about a dozen of us all started on the same day.

I had no idea what to expect but there was an even mix of boys and girls, some a little younger, some a little older.

The rules were elegant and simple – take inbound phone calls from people who had received Nynex marcoms (marketing and communications) material and were keen to find out about lower telephone costs and about 50 new sports, docos and news channels.

From the moment the red LCD board lit up at 9am and told us all there were calls waiting, I hit the answer button on my desk phone and didn't stop talking for the rest of the day. You could accurately say that was the day I slammed into drive.

I found the conversations easy and free-flowing and being from a humble background I totally related to their reasons for wanting to switch from the overpriced low-feature incumbent operator, British Telecom (BT).

That first day flew by and I don't think I even stopped for lunch. Stats weren't kept much in the early days but I knew from the stack of paper contracts that had taken over my desk I'd had a good haul, especially looking around at the quantity on my fellow colleagues' desks.

This carried on for a few weeks in the same vein and soon a simple whiteboard was set up to start tracking conversion ratios of calls to completed contracts that were then posted out.

There was a sales administration girl who was ace at collating all the data, so on the introduction of the whiteboard and figures being released for the first time the whole team stopped what they were doing and watched every red pen stroke.

Lo and behold, first cab off the rank was yours truly, Philip Hills. I can't remember exactly what my numbers were but I was clearly in first place and some of the other sales tigers were clearly a bit put out ... and that's when the politics started.

I've never been a political animal as I've always let my numbers do the talking for me.

The trend continued for some weeks and as I wasn't too bothered about 'hanging out' with my colleagues at lunch and too busy at my desk selling, the obvious rivalry just went over my head.

The Nynex marketing machine continued to push on as new areas continued to come online and the calls kept increasing, along with my quota.

Within months the team had grown yet again, and we moved to new offices.

The department now occupied a whole floor of the rather functional building but at least it had windows.

We were now split into teams or more accurately shifts – 8.30–4.30 / 10.30–6.30 / 12.30–8.30.

There were no targets per se but you got paid on your contracts signed and the team leader benefited from their team's efforts. Three teams, one per shift on a rotating basis and roughly eight per team from memory.

Certain shifts had certain benefits from both a work and social perspective. For example, the early shift was ideal for when they had just done a campaign on TV or print media the day before as everyone just jumped straight on the phone the next morning to get signed up.

The middle shift was awesome for your social life as rocking up to work at 10.30am was a summer breeze even if you'd had a big night. No rush-hour traffic in the morning, decent sleep-in and no evening traffic to battle with. If you lived in Brighton, there were nights out every day of the week if you wanted them and even if you weren't out, sitting around if you were staying in with your housemates in the stoner zone until late into the night was also a very popular option for a lot of people my age. Sales on this middle shift at work were still okay as you picked up the evening customers who had just got in from work and wanted information from any ads they had seen during the day. The evening shift was again great for social life and sales were still good because you got all the customers who had come home from work later and wanted to sign up before they settled down for the night.

I vaguely recall that Saturdays were introduced at some point and you got an extra day off during the week as compensation.

There were three types of contracts a customer could opt for: telephone only, cable TV only or combo. No guesses for what that might be.

Telephone was popular as your line rental was a lot less than BT, which at the time was exorbitant as they were the incumbent operator and had a captive market and charged like a wounded bull. Number portability wasn't an option initially but again, by being a bit ingenious and an inquisitive sort of chap, I'd found my way round the data-entry program and the screen with all the available telephone numbers, so I'd have a chat with the customer and find a number they liked. It worked a charm. I'd say something like, 'Look, if you sign up now, I'll allocate this number to you which I shouldn't really do, but if I do it quickly no one will know.'

Number portability was less of an issue if you were moving to a new house. Say, to a new area as even BT would have to give you a new number then anyway. So those customers were fair game. Plus, the install price was less than relocating a BT line.

TV I found an easy sell too as everyone wanted the sports and movies at a lower price than Sky and you didn't have to have a silly looking satellite dish installed on your roof. Although, having said that, at the time it was a bit of a status symbol to have a dish on your roof to show the neighbours you were cashed up to spend 30 quid a month on extra TV channels.

On the subject of price, I was made aware of the 'reduce it to the ridiculous' sales technique. It's used a lot in mainstream advertising, insurance in particular, but I didn't realise people actually fell for it. So, if the price was as in this case 30 pounds a month, you simply say one pound a day. Everyone had a pound a day they spend on unnecessary items, so the justification became relatable.

A combo I found really easy to sell but for some reason a lot of my colleagues didn't. Install fee was the same, whether you took TV or telephone, but I'd found a clause in the contract that meant you could cancel TV within 30 days. You couldn't do that with phone though. So, it was a piece of cake to up-sell from a telephone enquiry (which they mostly were) to a combo, which doubled your sales figures. At the end of each day the simple tally system on the whiteboard we used was filled with combos under my name. You actually went up to the board and did it yourself ... let's just say I was up at the board a lot and my colleagues were getting more and more irate.

The combo section, which counted as two sales, I was tallying up quite nicely in. For comparison, while most people in the department would struggle to hit double figures, I was hitting five combos (which meant 10 sales) plus a good spread of TV and telephone-only sales, which translated to about 20 per day. More than twice the average for the department.

When the teams were chosen, who decided who went where I don't know, but the top performers were all separated to give an even spread.

I settled into my team quickly and was performing best in my team and department overall.

A couple of the other sales guns who frankly rated themselves quite highly were starting to get seriously annoyed.

I recall a guy, Alex Sinclair, an ex-insurance salesman who wore lace-up shoes and a pressed white shirt with a properly knotted tie. He really had me in his crosshairs. I wore loafers, undone top button, my shirt sleeves rolled up, a loosely fitted tie – and I was outperforming him.

He also had a mate – Kevin, I think his name was – who worked there, and they played the crusty old good cop, bad cop routine on me.

'Oh, what corners are you cutting to get such good figures?'

'Hey Phil, would love to know how you're working to be doing so well.'

I was a kid who'd been knocking around the streets of Brighton for the last few years, so dealing with these clowns was like taking candy from a baby.

My MO was simple. Sell the benefits to the customer as quick as you could. Have a stack of blank contracts on your desk with some prefilled info already done and then do a proper contract in my own time after my shift had finished. Every time I looked round, Alex and his mate were sat deep in conversation, looking like they were trying to sell ice to eskimos. Nodding sagely at all the right times and generally taking it way too seriously.

I don't think I sat down at any point during the day. Motion creates emotion and all that.

Month after month I topped the leader board and when the time came to shift team members around, team leaders wanted me on their team and the one that had me fought tooth and nail to keep me.

A neat trick I learnt early on was that not all addresses were in the database. Which meant you couldn't book an install, which meant a contract couldn't be finalised, which in turn meant no stat until it was. There was a poorly laid-out, time-consuming form you could fill out and leave in a tray that someone in another department nearby would eventually get round to entering. Or, if you were enterprising enough or just used some common sense, walk next door, get friendly with the girls in data entry and get them to do it there and then. Et *voilà*, another sale.

Another smart little comms (commission) boosting use of time I happened to find out whilst chatting with one of the back of house girls was that a certain key, say F5 – remember these were all DOS-based terminals back then, in fact the only PC we had in the entire dept was with the sales admin girls – got you onto the install team's booking schedule. It was a major breakthrough that I naturally kept to myself, as it allowed you to book an install there and then and provided you knew the type of product they had taken – telco only, TV only or combo – you could pretty much guarantee a sale as there was not the to-and-fro phonecalls with the install team who might not be so accommodating with the client.

In all my years of sales, one of the things that has stayed with me is that time is the biggest killer of any potential deal. Don't leave to someone else what you can do yourself.

Finally, there was this great system they used for averages if you were off training, sick, annual leave or had an extra Saturday owing to you. Whenever there was any training there were always complaints that it was time away from the phone, so they devised a system where basically your average daily quota would be awarded to you even if you weren't there. For me and a few others it meant even when going on holiday, we earned good money. Looking back, we had it so good. I haven't been in a sales job since that offered such great incentives.

My salary was through the roof and my stock was trading high. I bought myself a new classic sportscar (MGB Roadster) without even having to sell my old Spitfire, so I now owned two cars to boot.

I got my housemate a job there and whilst he wasn't killing it sales-wise, he did okay and enjoyed the extra money as much as I did. We worked out how to be on the same shifts and save money by sharing petrol costs. Win–win again.

There was also a direct (door to door) sales force housed within the building and they soon got wind of some of the tele sales commission numbers and started taking a big interest in me and a few other high performers. There were always snide, gobby comments from them about being the real salesmen, and we were just pushy tele-sales amateurs. These were the type of guys who wore gold chains and way too much cheap-smelling cologne, so in reality they just made me laugh.

Probably down to internal tension both in the department and the business, one day we were all called to a team meeting. They never happened, so it sounded alarm bells. We were told we were only to get paid comms on actual installs, not contracts sent. Made sense and I never thought for one moment it would impact me. I wasn't the pushy kind of guy and knew the customers were dead-set keen on the offering.

It sent shockwaves through the department and scared the hell out of everyone.

Our ever-reliable sales admin girl put the numbers up on the whiteboard at the end of the month showing the new conditions of sales targets and everyone stopped and ogled at them. It was hilarious, my actual installs were higher than my contracts sent;

not a numerical error, just some missed installs because I had sold so much from previous months they were finally getting connected.

I was top of this list too and my team leader and overall manager could not have been happier. I expect even they thought I was going to come unstuck.

By now not just comms was being awarded but a President's Club scheme was open to us that the direct sales were part of and a special voucher system with a magazine of goodies to choose from. Let's just say I never had to buy a Christmas or birthday present all the time I was working there and was looking forward to my all-expenses paid trip to Hawaii.

The team continued to grow, and I was asked if I wanted to be a team leader due to my performance. It put a lot of people's noses out, but the salary was awesome and I knew it was a great step forward as I now considered myself to have a career not just a job, so I said all the right things to the manager and got the job.

Bear in mind that being a great salesperson doesn't always equate to being good at managing sales people. There were a few people in the department who clearly thought they had more managerial potential than some sportscar-driving, loafer-wearing wordsmith in his mid-20s. More recruitment was done and my team (now four teams in total) was a mix of original team members and newbies.

My style of leadership has always been one of lead by example. I never quite got to read the manual or textbook on leadership if there was one. I wanted to see practical examples of how the theory is applied.

I got myself a double headphone jack, listened in on their calls and helped steer them through the art of the sales process. If they were off for the day, I would happily jump on the phone and book sales in their names. What's good for the goose is also good for the gander and all that. It showed I was there to help them as most of the other team leaders were just off gossiping over by the kitchen, looking for any opportunity to skive off doing anything resembling productive work. All the little tricks I'd picked up along the way I happily shared.

So effective was this strategy on the first month of me being a team supervisor we topped the charts for the next few months until a bombshell was dropped.

As the age-old well-worn saying goes: all good things must end.

Another rare department meeting was called and we were told that the telesales operations were to be relocated to Manchester where the network build-out was going to be bigger and generate higher revenue for the company. In some ways we had been so successful, the penetration levels were so high that the ROI (return on investment) wasn't looking as attractive for the company.

It blindsided all of us and there were gasps and tears, but I'd known it wasn't sustainable and had been busily saving the extra cash (mainly to get a deposit together to buy a flat – which I managed in about six months but which ultimately fell through) and taken the promotion, so it put me in good stead for the next step. I just didn't know the next step would come so soon.

Then an unexpected thing happened after the meeting. Celia, the overall department manager, took me and a couple of others aside and asked us if we would like to relocate up North. All expenses paid, bit of a promotion, bit more cashola ... all looked good on paper at least.

As amazing as the offer was – a lot of my mates had gone to university up North so I knew it had a good party scene and there was plenty of fun to be had, plus it was much cheaper to live there – but I just wasn't in the headspace to leave my beloved Brighton. I'd recently got into a serious relationship and the timing wasn't right for me. I was in drive mode, remember – and there was still a lot of work to be done right where I was.

For the next few hours and days, it was all anyone spoke about. Those with a bit of schadenfreude would stop me and say, 'Ah, bad luck, Phil, just as you got the team leader position, things have all gone pear-shaped.'

I couldn't have agreed less ... I knew I had found my calling career-wise and wasn't going to waste any more sweet precious time in life.

The sales admin girl who had always had my back from the start, I expect mainly due to the fact she knew how many people were gunning to take me down, offered her PC skills to put together a curriculum vitae for me. What the hell was one of those? I'd only ever filled out application forms for jobs and knew nothing of this other corporate world that existed.

What she presented to me a few days later was nothing short of spectacular. My work life beautifully presented with a double line border on one side of an A4 piece of paper, including all my notable achievements from Nynex expertly laid out. Remember, we only had dumb DOS terminals at the time and no one had a computer at home to learn Word or Excel, so there was no sneakily doing your thing during work time.

Even I was impressed with what I'd achieved when it was all laid out and I already knew I was top dog ... woof woof. As a lovely cherry on top, I was given an ex-gratia payment of 1500 pounds for the President's Club trip to Hawaii I would have been going on, in recognition of my performance. It was literally raining cash on me.

The relationship I had recently got into was with a lovely girl who I met from knocking around Brighton; she was part of the scene and one night we got talking and instead of the usual chat about music, drugs, clubs and bars, I found myself talking about my job situation. Brighton has a rich history of, shall we say, 'illegitimate businessmen' – antique dealers, property developers, car salesmen, drug dealers and your general chancers in life. In everyday parlance, you would call these nefarious characters 'dodgy geezers'.

I think she appreciated a break from the usual well-worn topics of conversation and very soon we discovered we had a lot in common. Suz was at uni at the time and studying a business degree with a view to getting into an advertising career in London.

We soon started going steady and my newfound promotion (however short-lived) gave us a great standard of living where we dined at nice restaurants, cruised around in my MGB and generally had a lot of fun.

Then it came time to meet the parents. I knew Suz was from an affluent area of Brighton – if you've ever read any Peter James books, I strongly suggest you do, he constantly refers to the place as wherever there is money there are always good stories.

Anyway, I went around for drinks and met her mum and dad. The house was pretty impressive. I've always liked the idea of a gravel carriage driveway. Tick. Double fronted – tick. Spacious garage – tick.

We had drinks on the rear deck overlooking the parklands and conversation flowed easily. For some reason I've always enjoyed speaking to other people's parents and after the initial trial by 100 questions from Mum and Dad we fell into an easy groove and talked about all things and everything. It turned out we shared a love of skiing, cars and sport.

John was clearly a captain of industry and enjoyed the trappings of his success and wasn't ashamed to share them. It quickly transpired that he too had a very successful career in telecoms and had held very senior positions in BT, the very company I was in competition with. Suz explained I was leading the President's Club program, had recently been promoted but now faced the agonising choice of my next career move with the department being relocated.

Anyway, (LSS) long story short, John was now a consultant in the telecoms industry as MD of a start-up backed by the billionaire Estée Lauder's empire, and they were looking to grow the company rapidly here in the UK.

Deregulation of the telecoms industry was happening in the UK, which is how Nynex got their licence to operate, and a lot of other American firms (where deregulation had already taken place years earlier) were keen to get a foothold in a country that had a decent-sized, relatively affluent population. So, although Estée Lauder was a cosmetics company, they knew it was good business and highly profitable to get into telecoms. So RSL (Ronald Steven Lauder) Telecom was born.

The drill was simple – take customers off BT with lower rates, run an efficient operation. Get the EBITDA looking respectable and list on the Nasdaq. Watch the share price rise and make off like a bandit with millions and millions of dollars.

A lot of British industries ended up with competition from private enterprise and as well as BT, British Rail, British Gas and the postal service, which were all bloated, inefficient and hamstrung by trade unions, were easy targets for astute businessmen to come and eat their proverbial lunch business-wise. These sectors were badly in need of investment, so the government was more than happy to take licence fees and let others clean up the mess from years of neglect.

John told me that RSL needed a sales manager to run their telesales department: would I be interested in looking further into it? Er, you bet your sweet cotton socks I would! 'Would you like to see my CV?' I asked. It impressed him immensely – it was one impressive CV for a 25-year-old.

The saying 'When opportunity knocks, don't complain about the noise' was written for this exact occasion.

Apparently, the words 'President's Club' are like manna from heaven in the corporate world of sales and I'd just unknowingly got myself in the fast lane of a highway that I would power down for many years to come as a result. Problem was, I was running on the wrong type of fuel and 20 years later, unbeknown to me, that fuel I was using would blow the motor (i.e. brain cancer).

Interviews were quickly arranged and in no time at all I found myself in a 30K-a-year job in charge of a whole department. Well, again it was a department of one – me – but it was my job to build it and grow that line of business from the ground up, which I did very swiftly.

I took off at 100 miles per hour and never looked in the rearview mirror ever again ... until now.

True to form, RSL Com built up a very successful business, not just in the UK but all over Europe. We soon moved to a lovely European HQ in a wonderful town called Guildford and, given the fact that I was probably one of the first ten people to work there, I had a spot in the building's car park – this meant no time-consuming parking on the street which could be especially unappealing in the depths of an English winter.

However, it wasn't all that straightforward and the job came with many challenges.

———⚜———

CHAPTER 10

Playing with the Big Boys

The Cure – Boys Don't Cry (1980)

In this chapter, my life takes me from my comfort blanket of sleepy small towns to big city life.

M Y FIRST ROLE on joining before we set up the telesales department was to last a couple of months. I was tasked with setting up the sales support function of the direct sales team at the Old Street office where we had our NOC (Network Operations Centre) and Switch. This was basically where we interconnected with the BT network to offer all the RSL services. This was based in London and my first proper commuting job up in 'Town', as those who did the daily trip to London would snobbily call it. It was a bit of humble brag if you like. Interestingly, when I met Mel, she would call the city (in Sydney) town as well but that was a country thing and no bragging at all.

I caught the train at 7.30am from Preston Park with all the other city slickers and then got the underground across town from Victoria Station to Old Street Station. It was about one and a half hours all up but I loved it. All I'd ever done in the past was sit in my car to get to work and whilst l loved driving, reading a book or paper or having an hour's sleep sure beat that.

The direct sales team were a force of nature. They'd been recruited wholesale from another company called Worldcom who did what RSL was doing now but a year or so earlier.

These guys were machines. To hear them on the phone and set up appointments with clients who they admittedly already knew from their time at Worldcom had to be seen to be believed. They were quite a bit older than me ... I would have been about 25 at the time and these blokes – six of them in their early 30s – had all worked together along with their sales manager for the last few years.

Their sales patter was so well oiled, it was hard not to be impressed with them. They were a slick performing unit that was as tight as two coats of paint. As individuals though, they were complete assholes.

My job was to help them process the printed bills they got from clients – large multi-national corporations with big international spend on their bills – and compare them using RSL rates to their current provider, be it BT or Worldcom, who were really the only two players in the market.

The fabulous CV that had been put together by the sales admin girl l spoke about earlier had accurately said that l was using Excel and Word to collate daily sales figures. What it did not say was that l had advanced skills in VLOOKUP data in cross-referencing and formulas, which l didn't!

I had to scan double-sided phone bills, clean the data, then use that info to cross-reference a database of tariffs from existing suppliers.

It wasn't a simple case of just filling in a couple of cells with a one or two-digit number and letting the table do the math. l had to write a set of very complex formulas.

May this be a warning about what you put on your resume; ensure it is true, as it may come back to haunt you! I hadn't overstated mine but I was playing with the big boys now and they had expectations. Anyway, I picked it up quickly enough but not quickly enough for some of the direct sales guys to see a chink in my armour and go for the jugular. These guys, remember, saw me as someone punching above his weight. They believed I was just there because of who my girlfriend was, rather than getting the job on merit. They were animals and trained to seize any opportunity to gain an advantage, whether it be with clients in the outside world or internally within the organisation. I distinctly remember the sales manager Steve Burgess saying to me, 'We play to win, Phil' about something trivial like whose turn it was to get a round of tea in.

Once I had the spreadsheets mastered and the guys got their proposals back so they could revisit the client and win the business over from the competitor, the digs started coming. Keith Weaver, I think it was, came over and said something like, 'Not bad for someone who got the job because he's going out with (replace with stronger language) the MD's daughter.'

He made sure he said it in earshot of the other sales guys, and they all gave a hearty roar of laughter. I couldn't believe what I was hearing and from that moment the mood between me and the direct sales team changed. I did all the work they asked me to, but they would just dump the bills on my desk and say things like, 'Don't tell the boss how long I was out for lunch.'

We had our official launch of the company and Suz came along. These guys, some who had partners and some who didn't, were right in there, being really slimy with her, trying to get a reaction from me in front of the entire company. Fortunately, for all the faults I have jealously is not a trait I've ever possessed, and I wasn't about to start now.

Suz, who was a very attractive young lady, was lapping up the attention, but she knew what they were up to and dealt with it with pure class. Unfortunately, due to the nature of these guys, all it achieved was to stir them up into making more obvious moves on her at future work events. Even with her dad as MD of the company, these fellas knew no limits. They got away with it though because by God they could sell, and I got to see how in the corporate world being the flashiest, smoothest and most outrageous earned you respect. All the ultimate big bosses wanted was revenue every month to make the balance sheet look good. To be fair, John (Suz's dad) wasn't complicit in giving these guys an easy time of their behaviour but as he was only MD on a consultant basis and the CEO (who he reported to) and him went way back at BT, they knew the rules of engagement.

Soon they got a girl called Tracy (also ex Worldcom) to do the support job full-time and my time in London was over. It was back to the safe sanctuary of the lovely Guildford European HQ just outside London.

They did eventually work me over and get the better of me however. We had our official companywide launch party down in the Cotswolds and because the company was doing so well it was a lavish affair with partners invited. We were there all day Saturday and at the evening event the guys from direct sales, whether they had their partner there or not, were spreading the compliments onto Suz nice and thick. While I was networking with other people from the company, they all took it in turn to surround her and try and get a reaction. It was like dealing with a tag team of wrestlers when you are fighting on your own. By the end of the night, with all the bars closed and even the hardiest partiers all but done for, we retreated to our rooms. I was exhausted as it had been a big night of networking whilst having one eye over my shoulder, looking out for Suz. These guys were animals!

As we were about to drift off (or at least I thought that was happening), Suz asked why I hadn't been giving her any attention like all the other guys had. I really wasn't in the mood for having to justify myself and probably didn't handle the situation as well as I should have, and an almighty row broke out at 3am. Long story short: I got the serious hump, got dressed and left the room and the hotel. It was the middle of the night in a deserted village in the middle of the Cotswolds and I had to somehow find my way back to Brighton, still drunk but with a hangover starting to kick in from the night's activities.

I somehow found my way to the nearest train station and through blurry eyes worked out that the next train to anywhere wasn't for another good few hours.

Money wasn't really an object back then, so I managed to flag down a passing taxi and he nearly fainted when I asked him the fare to Brighton, which was almost halfway across the other side of the country. We agreed, the fare went via a cashpoint to secure the deal and I settled back into the seat for what would be at least a three to four-hour cab ride.

I remember it distinctly – to be fair who wouldn't, it had been a night to remember and it was still only 4am – but it was the night Bruno fought Tyson for their rematch and being in the US it was on live for most of the journey home. Ultimately, Bruno lost but it was a welcome distraction for the build-up and for the few short rounds it lasted. Obviously, being the gentleman I am (ahem), I left Suz the car and with it the front door keys so all in all I'd got myself into a bit of a pickle. I knew my parents always had a spare key hidden under a strategically placed pot and as they lived quite nearby, I elected to go back there, let myself in as it would be around 7 to 8am by then to get some sleep and deal with the nuclear fallout that would undoubtedly follow on Sunday. But right now I needed to find a bed, and this was by far the best option. In fact, the reason it was the best option was because, if you hadn't already guessed, it was my only option.

Meanwhile back in the Cotswolds, Suz had to wake to explain (I'm still not sure exactly what she said) why I wasn't there at the breakfast the next morning.

Unfortunately, cracks had already started to appear in our otherwise perfect relationship. We had a lovely mews townhouse, we both had great jobs and a great social life, but things in the new house didn't get off to a great start. Or should I say the reason for buying it was a bit conflicted.

At the time we met, I was living in a shared house in Hollingbury, an area just on the outskirts of Brighton town centre. It was with another two guys and one girl and the house had an easy rhythm to it; for after-parties and such like I had mates who lived nearer the town centre and that's where most of the mess and mayhem happened.

Suz, by contrast, owned her own two-bedroom flat in a lovely leafy suburb called Preston Park, just down the road from me. I say Suz owned it but in truth her dad had bought it for her and used it as an investment property, whereby the plan was for Suz to rent out the spare room to cover the mortgage. It was a smart idea but in reality Suz opted to live there alone and I'm sure John wasn't too bothered about forgoing the small contribution, as property was so cheap back then in Brighton and the mortgage was not large. Anyway, it wasn't long until the money I'd saved at Nynex began burning a hole in my pocket as property prices started to gain momentum.

It was during the whole buy-to-let period and it quickly transpired you could make a decent wage by buying a couple of properties and living off the profit from the rental income. I wasn't interested in making money from the rent, but the rising tide of property prices was enticing to me and since my property purchase had fallen through a year or so earlier, I was keen to get back into the market. I told Suz of my wishes and to my astonishment she was less than pleased, quite frankly annoyed at why I didn't want to buy with her. We were young and hadn't really spoken about kids or marriage at all, so it wasn't like I was stealing her future dreams from her.

Buying a place with Suz really hadn't crossed my mind, as I knew the place she was living in was going to be given to her by her dad ultimately.

But it did make sense to pool our resources and get something bigger, so we started looking at getting a joint mortgage. We soon settled on this delightful mews cottage over three floors with three bedrooms, three bathrooms and a garage. It was ideal. Just around the corner from Hove Station where Suz would commute from, as she now had finished her uni course and starting her career in London.

I remember John got involved in the negotiations, which wasn't unwelcome, and asked how much I was putting in as a deposit, as he was going to match me pound for pound. I told him how much I had saved and think he was kinda surprised at the large amount, but he was a man of many means and said, 'Okay, no problem we're going 50/50.' I then told him that in fact I didn't want to go all in and wanted to keep some of my powder dry. He was a little shocked by this and told me that the more you put in, the less interest you are charged and ultimately the less it costs. I knew this of course but my parents didn't have deep pockets like John and if anything went wrong I would need rainy day funds. I've always been very shrewd when it comes to savings as I hate the notion of not having money. A deep-rooted insecurity that at the time I was not sure where it came from, but I suspect it was often hearing my parents complain about money and me recognising I never wanted my life to be like that. I also knew I couldn't rely on them to bail me out if things went pear-shaped.

John accepted that it was probably a prudent move and I suspect he was secretly a bit impressed that I was so sensible with money, despite being in a good financial position.

Life was great for a year or so and now Suz was really enjoying working in London. Enjoying herself a little too much, it would seem. I didn't really see it unfolding as I was caught up in my own career but regular stayovers in London were starting to happen with her team members – until one day the apparently inevitable happened. We attempted to continue our relationship after this event, including the tried-and-tested holiday to rekindle what we had left, but this failed miserably. I ended up doing the same playing-away game in return, which marked the end. John bought me out of the place and Suz stayed there for several more years. The person I then met ended up being my next long-term girlfriend.

So back to where I was placed for work ...

Guildford is a beautiful market town in Surrey with a great high street, lots of parks and fields, and great bars and restaurants. It was about an hour's drive from where I lived in Brighton. By this point I'd upgraded my MGB (but still owned it) and bought myself a relatively modern though still a few years old BMW 3 Series. It was a sporty model with upgraded suspension and fancy interior and the cross-country drive was a real hoot every day to and from work.

As I've mentioned, due to the fact that I was one of the first to join, I got a space in the car park out the front of the building but gradually, as more and more senior people joined the various business functions, this became a problem as the obviously limited spaces became ever more hotly contested. Meanwhile, the 'lowly' telesales manager was not considered worthy of such a spot. What is it with people and telesales!? That they think they are a superior species to us? We are an extremely low-cost, highly efficient method of generating revenue that is scalable and flexible if the market dynamic changes. We're not selling time share or burglar alarms to poor old unsuspecting pensioners.

I suspect most people thought my car spot was because of my relationship with the MD's daughter. It was a conclusion I was growing a little tired of. I needn't have worried though as after I'd been there nearly a year John had a major falling out with some very senior executives at the company and as he was a consultant, he was there one day and gone the next. Simple as that.

He did explain the reason for it to me and it was due to a disagreement in strategy about how to grow the business. All well above my paygrade and since my telesales department was cranking along and delivering some fine numbers I didn't mind that my protector, as everyone assumed, was gone. Just like at Nynex, I let my numbers do the talking. I was now becoming very adept at talking about EBITDA (earnings before interest, taxes, depreciation and amortisation), run rates and gross margin and I knew my numbers well enough that, if anyone arced up on me, I very quickly reminded them of my department's figures and they soon backed off. As it turned out, my biggest threat was to come from someone in my own team. The enemy within!!

I was overall manager of a team of about 20. We had a couple of shifts and consequently a couple of supervisors to manage these teams, in relation to making sure we had coverage seven days a week as well as helping out with tricky customers.

Jan, I seem to remember her name was, was that very enemy within. She desperately wanted my job, and she took no time in undermining me and setting her sights on my desk.

She was or became good friends with the HR manager. They would have their little gossip breaks together and then slowly, slowly they decided to build a negative profile of me within the business. White-anting I think the modern-day term is ... in other words, a subtle form of sabotage.

Meanwhile I was collating huge amounts of data from call logs within the platform so we could see where the main telecom routing profile of customers was and adjust rates accordingly. This was so we could remain competitive and ensure we were profitable. Both very important aspects of running the business. I learnt how to build Access databases (a Microsoft program like Excel) to comb this data and present it in reports, not only to my director but the senior executives above him. Fraud was also a big issue in this type of business, so to identify a cluster of calls where the originating number was the same was very important. In order to charge a prepaid calling card, a credit card was often used, very often a stolen credit card. And we had to identify those phone cards as the financial institution would dishonour the transaction via a system called 'charge back'. By identifying a cluster of calls we could pinpoint where the fraudulent activity originated from. I was the only person in the company who'd learnt how to extract this kind of data for our platform until later a great guy called Paul Jeffries took a promotion to fraud manager across the whole business. I became very good friends with Paul during the three years I worked at RSL. He was close in age, good fun to be around and not a political animal or climber of the greasy career pole. I have a lot to thank Paul for due to some professional colleagues he introduced me to, who helped with a financial predicament I was in at the time. A story I will tell in due course.

Learning how to do mail merges from the proprietary software we had adapted to house the now many thousands of customers we had was also very useful in managing the marketing side of our business unit. Jan thought all this computer stuff was a waste of time and if you weren't visible sitting with the staff doing pointless surveys and performance reviews then you weren't managing the department effectively. I had the support of my director who had run a similar business before joining RSL and he was only interested in the numbers (and the girls who worked in the call centre, but more on that shortly) in terms of run rate of minutes and how much revenue we were generating. Really the only two numbers a telecoms business like ours looks at.

My director was a veteran of the industry and a great guy, but he did have shortcomings and that was he couldn't keep his hands off the young girls who worked in the teams. I had numerous females come to me and say he was being creepy, lewd and generally what I would describe as a bit of a pervert.

After a departmental party the situation came to a head and one of the young girls told me what he'd done and I had no choice but to raise it with him. I said I would deal with him directly. We got on well, she trusted me and said okay, no problem.

After I told him in no uncertain terms to 'stop thinking with the wrong head', our relationship changed for the worse. As you can imagine, doing that went down like a grit sandwich and what had once been a close amicable working relationship quickly changed.

I can't remember exactly the course of events, but it went something like this.

Jan, my team leader, got wind of the event and told her HR buddy. My director, trying to cover his arse, got HR involved and said it was just a misunderstanding. I was dragged over the coals for failing to let HR know about a sexual misconduct complaint. The whole thing got bigger than Ben Hur and with him being a director and with the HR director involved and Jan her mate wanting my job, I was the meat in the sandwich and got put in a very difficult position. That difficult position very quickly turned into a new position in my own department. They knew that John was now out of the picture, so this was their opportunity to strike. I was told Jan would now be running the department and that my director would take some much-needed time off as he had been doing long hours and needed stress leave.

I was told I would be moved to just work on the analytics side of the business and not be involved in the day-to-day running of the department, which I had built from the ground up to be a very successful channel of revenue for the company. I couldn't believe it. I flat-out refused to leave my desk at the front of the department.

It caused a few problems and I was summoned up to see the CEO, Richard Williams.

Richard, along with John, had essentially started the company and they knew each other from their BT days. He was an older gent, very tall, wiry with grey hair and had long since lost his very executive look and feel. He very graciously offered me a seat in his office and said how grateful he was for the fine work I'd done in building the department. He was aware of how much John respected me and that it was unfortunate he had to leave. He was aware of the situation in the department and since I had been there almost as long as him, he thought it was time I took a promotion and started the roll out of Global Phone around Europe. I had the knowledge and skills to carry out the plan and would be managed by a guy called Terry and work in a satellite office down the road with all the other European managers.

I couldn't believe it. It was ideal. Travel around Europe on the company doing what I knew and loved, and once again adding a notch to my CV bedpost. I would be relocated to a smaller office in the heart of Guildford town centre, which was a great location to work and I could expense my parking. It was perfect and it meant I could get away from the political busybodies who were looking to climb and winch themselves up the career pole and leave me the hell alone. My first day there I walked in and saw lots of familiar faces from the European HQ who I assumed had left but had in fact gone on to more specialist roles in the company. It wasn't busy that often as most of the time we were out in the other European cities where we had operations – in France, Germany and Austria to name but a few.

My new boss Terry was a consultant from the network of the old BT staff that John and Richard knew, and he was never in the office, so I just came and went as I pleased and flew business class around Europe the majority of the week. My only real concern was how long it was going to take me to get from Bronze Frequent Flyer to Gold so I could start getting enough points for free flights. I put my head down and got on with the job of getting the European versions of Global Phone rolled out.

Now would be a good time to retell that story of a chance meeting with a couple of guys Paul (from the fraud team I mentioned) and I had lunch with. Paul was a good friend by now and was always popping into the European satellite office a few days a week to say hi as he was also good friends with a guy called Kevin, who looked after the business analytics of the same countries I was rolling out Global Phone into. He was a bit of a spreadsheet jockey with his uni degree or some MBA he might have had, but he was good value nonetheless and was a down-to-earth guy who I also got on with.

The back story here is that true to form, RSL had built up a very successful business and were ready for their IPO (initial public offering) on the Nasdaq. For those of us that had been there a while there were some very attractive share offer opportunities to be had. Basically, the max you could buy was a block of 5,000 shares at pre-IPO price (say $1). We were going through a tech bubble globally, so the shares would invariably rise on launch and some very good money was to be made.

I bought my max allowance of my first-ever foray into the world of share dealing and waited. I've never been a sophisticated investor and have done very well financially in life by following the simple maxim of spending less than you earn. I've always bought my cars cash and never had car loans or any kind of loan other than a mortgage. Again, I think it's to do with my upbringing where I never learnt any financial savvy from my parents as they didn't have spare money to play with.

By this time Suz had got a position at Reuters, the global news agency. Her job was to sell their services and content to companies that could benefit from up-to-date news and share price/ exchange rate indices. Remember, the internet wasn't as prevalent as it is today.

Suz had access to live share prices and set up an alert on the RSL share code on her software and I made a deal with myself I would sell when the price doubled my money. Sure enough, the share price rose on debut and continued its upward trend and after a few weeks was up about 50–60 per cent. Good going but not the double bubble I was waiting on. It continued to climb and then one day it hit the magic double milestone. Suz got the alert on her Reuters software and called me.

I had a Nokia mobile phone back in the day (the 6210 everyone had) but they were notorious for being poor on battery life and for whatever reason I didn't have a charger in the car. It was about 6pm and Suz guessed she could just tell me when I got home around 7pm. Being listed on the Nasdaq and therefore in New York meant it was open for a good few hours into the UK evening.

I got in and Suz gave the great news that the price had doubled, so I picked up the phone to place a sell order. Merrill Lynch were underwriting the IPO and everyone who bought shares had been given an info pack on the offer. I rang the number, got through to someone who was manning the evening desk and explained who I was and what I wanted to do. This guy tried for what seemed like an eternity to find my account so he could book a sale but just couldn't find a trace of RSL or my name so he couldn't book the sell order. He said he'd ask around and give me a call back. Which after about 20 minutes he did and said the whole team were flummoxed and at a loss and could it wait until the morning. There were only a few hours till closing on the Nasdaq and the stock was still trending upwards.

By now it was around 9 or 10pm UK time and I was ready for bed, so I said yeah, no problem, let's wait until all the back of house are in tomorrow and get it sorted. I went to bed that night dreaming about what I might spend my five grand on.

When I woke the next morning I put on the little portable TV we had in the bedroom and there, splashed all over the news was: 'Major earthquake in Japan, global stock markets taking a hammering.' I simply couldn't believe it. Suz looked at her laptop and sure enough, all markets were deep in the red and of course RSL was well down. Well down, in fact. I lost all my profit and then some and if memory serves me right, they were now below IPO price. I did not enjoy my journey to work and got straight onto the phone to my man at Merrill Lynch. He had found the problem: because we had bought under a company account linked to the underwriting of the offer, mine and others were held in a separate part of the system which is why he hadn't been able to find my account. He was obviously inundated with calls from panicked clients and the only consolation was that he told me to sit tight as prices would rise again.

Little comfort to me or anyone else at RSL or around the world who had shares. I'll be totally honest: I gave little or no consideration for the unfortunate inhabitants of whatever prefecture the quake destroyed and buried under tons and tons of rubble. I was just annoyed about losing my 5K profit. But not only my 5K profit but also by now my original stake as prices continued to tank.

There were some glum faces around the office that day.

So as the days and weeks and months wore on, the price never did recover and it seemed like the dream had completely evaporated.

Until the day I met a couple of Paul's colleagues.

Not sure how it came up but anyway, the story was told in full and one of the guys said, 'Nah, that's not right, give the financial ombudsman a call and tell them what happened.'

We all finished our pints and went back to work and as you can imagine, I jumped straight on the phone and told them my story. Now, as luck would have it, as a perk of the job being connected through the RSL telephony network, we had free calls. I asked the guys in the Network Operations Centre to give me the call log from my house to the Merrill Lynch office to prove I made the call. I said that if Merrill Lynch checked their call logs, they would see a call back to me about 10 minutes after, thereby proving my account of what happened.

I knew it was a long shot but by then and with the share price at its current level, I had nothing to lose and everything to gain. Pretty sure Paul didn't buy into the share offer. I certainly didn't give the intel to anyone else.

Then, a few days later my phone rang, and the conversation went something like this.

'Hi, Phil speaking.'

'Hi Phil, it's Jemil here. I've just found out about your chat with the financial ombudsmen. How come you didn't call me?'

'I did,' came my reply, 'and you told me to just wait for the share price to rebound.' As it turns out, no one in the finance industry likes a call from the ombudsmen and his next line blew me away.

'Ah okay, yeah sure, I did say that, but I've spoken to my manager and he's prepared to make an exception in your case because there was a bit of confusion. If you accept the following offer, you'll have to sign a document that you won't disclose this information to anyone else, is that clear?'

'Crystal,' came my reply. 'If it's acceptable,' I followed up with. Jemil then said, 'Okay, so we'll agree to a sale of the shares at their high on that date and time and we'll send you a cheque, is that okay?'

Well, no prizes for guessing what my response was. The cheque for a touch over 10K duly arrived a few days later but being sworn to secrecy I couldn't tell anyone at work. Everyone who was in the program was still moping around and lamenting their losses, but I was riding high on my unbelievably fortuitous bit of good luck. I'm not sure what I even did with the money. I think I just used it to top up my rainy day fund that had taken a battering after buying the house.

I was also in hindsight starting to become more than a little obsessed with money and having enough of it to feel secure whilst at the same time spending up large on material possessions and a good lifestyle.

As a beautiful footnote to this era of my life, RSL had a very generous personal pension fund as part of the remuneration package when I started. I don't know if it was available to all staff, maybe only the early ones. A lot of the first guys to join were much older and near retirement age and there were attractive tax incentives to put part of your salary into the pension fund and then use it in a few years to help fund your retirement. I suspect it was set up to attract the guys who were at BT with Richard and John, but I couldn't say for certain. One guy – our finance director (Jim Owen, if I recall correctly) – was always rubbing his hands with glee when we spoke about the pension plan, but I thought nothing of it. But just recently I looked into cashing it in, due to my terminal illness, and almost to the pound it ended up being enough to pay for both my girls' private school fees for their entire time at high school. Incredible for a job I worked at for three years, and a great example of investing whilst you are young so the money can make money for you.

———ↄ⅏ↄ———

The Bright Lights of London's West End and Beyond

Pet Shop Boys – West End Girls (1984)

In this chapter I talk about how the tentacles of my Brighton life still had a hand in making the most life-changing event that ultimately led me to work all over the world. As I write this book, I work for a global Finnish furniture company.

L ET'S GO BACK a few steps though. My career took me some years to settle on, but it became clear to me it was the right path to follow. I had decided it was the new era of telecommunications that really spun my wheels. It was new, exciting, fast-paced and well paid. Telecoms, to give it its shorter name that everyone used. First a quick history lesson though. For many years the government of each developed country auctioned off what they called 'operating spectrum', which was basically a frequency you were allowed to operate telecommunications devices over. There were no mobile phones back then; 2G, 3G etc. would be developed later but these are all examples of the operating spectrum. Essentially, the government holds auctions to determine who gets the spectrum so they can operate. For many many years it was always the incumbent operator who was the licence holder, such as British Telecom in the UK, itself a by-product of the telegraph service from decades before it. There is a lot to talk about here but so as not to bore you out of your brackets I will give you the abridged version. Long story short, I was in the right place at the right time. More accident than by design, or so it seemed. There was phenomenal growth in this industry when I was in my mid to late 20s and as we have touched on in other chapters, I rode the wave like a pro surfer.

Let's fast forward to 2001 when I'm 30 years old and working for a global telecommunications company called GTS in the West End of London. I know it is 2001 as one of the benefits of LinkedIn is you can track your life back to exact dates, which has been very useful for the purposes of writing this book. It was also the timing of a major correction in the industry around late 2001, known now as the dot-com bubble. Before it hit, like most seismic shifts, there had been warnings or tremors. One of those warnings was that a lot of companies suddenly found themselves with no money as funding avenues started to evaporate. And here is how it played out for me, leading to my next big step in life.

I had made quite a name for myself at this company and became known as 'Formula 1 Phil'. The origins of this name make quite a story. One day just sitting working at my desk, at the time as European Network Development Manager, the phone rang and I answered with my normal response: 'Philip Hills, GTS Telecommunications.' On the other end of the line was a very gruff East End accent. He asked, 'Is that Philip Hills?' To which I replied, 'How can I help?' He proceeded to tell me he was Bernie Ecclestone's r-hand man. For those who may not know, he was at the time the numero supremo boss at the top of the Formula One empire.

His reputation carried a huge amount of weight. I had been working on another project with another company called International Communication Enterprises (ICE), who needed a European Network for its Moto GP branded calling cards. Calling cards had a number you dialled first and then entered a pin to receive cheap rates when calling internationally. Perfect for fans of Moto GP and Formula One (F1) as they travelled the world, as well as for your everyday international traveller, they were still around at the start of the rise of mobile phones. I had been introduced to the owners of the company in a roundabout sort of way at a trade fair. This company held the rights to market Moto GP and many famous riders like Max Biaggi. I worked closely with them to get their network up and running to support their branded calling cards. It turned out that due to the rumblings of the oncoming tech-stock bubble bursting as mentioned, which would in hindsight be called the dot-com bubble, money was evaporating across the industry as avenues to raise funds were drying up. The guy on the other end of the line was called Barry Silver and he had previous dealings with ICE who, incidentally, were starting to run out of money as well. They had been working on a similar branded calling card for Formula One. As the conversation flowed I became aware that Barry was losing confidence in ICE; he was keen to cut out the middle man and wondered if GTS who I was working for would be interested in taking on the project for F1. My boss at the time was a great guy called Peter who was to be a major influence in my life, including the start of what was to be my trek Down Under. I got on with him very well. He was Senior Vice President (SVP) of the department and after sharing the news with him, he was obviously very enthusiastic about it. Endless phone calls ensued between myself, Barry and Peter. Gradually, more and more people in the company became aware of this project that was offered to us, so much so that senior managers I was not even aware of would come down to my department, introduce themselves to me and ask how the F1 project was going. In the end, my immediate colleagues started referring to me as F1 Phil. I got the project as far as I could, including attending key board meetings to go through the fine detail of the project. Ultimately though GTS, my company, was also getting squeezed by the lack of finance. Bernie Ecclestone, who was one of the world's richest businessmen, knew how to extract money from businesses with regards to F1 licences and his fees for putting F1's name to this project became too exorbitant for my company to finance. So with that deal dead in the water with GTS, the only way that Barry could keep the F1 name on calling cards active was to put his faith back in ICE to keep the deal going. He had no choice. As I had been so involved in the project and knew it inside out, I was poached by ICE to work directly with Barry who I had now built quite a rapport with. ICE offered a very attractive salary along with the opportunity to travel the world with F1. I naturally jumped at the chance, as my company had gradually started laying people off due to the credit squeeze in the tech sector. This all happened in a matter of months.

Many, many years ago and totally unrelated to this book, other than me using the word now in the context of writing it, I was having a conversation with someone and they used the word 'serendipitous'. They weren't trying to be clever or show off in any way. It was just the perfect use of the word in the context of what we were talking about. I'll level with you here at this point and tell you after that encounter I actually looked it up as I wasn't totally sure of its meaning. My mum always told me not to use words you can't spell or know the meaning of. I'll explain it now so as to avoid any confusion and make her proud.

Serendipitous – the faculty or phenomenon of finding valuable or agreeable things not sought for.

So, with this definition in your mind and the tech-stock bubble in the process of bursting, ICE, the company where I had only just accepted an amazing job opportunity, was now also being affected. I suddenly found myself, having recently bought a flat in the picturesque London suburb of Kew and working for a company that had up until the month before or so been paying me a very handsome wage, out on a limb. No more wage. I wasn't overly worried – I had some decent cash reserves on hand as I always did and my then girlfriend worked in the same industry but in an area that wasn't as affected as mine, so there wasn't any immediate cause for concern. However, after yet another missed pay cheque and a lot of horror stories starting to surface, it was squeaky bum time. One particular day, I needed to make a call to my mate's girlfriend – don't worry, nothing juicy to get from this – so I stepped outside. It wasn't a call I particularly wanted to make as the topic was sensitive (again, nothing juicy here). Someone was accusing her of stealing money – I knew this not to be true and I said as such to the person accusing her, but then this was turned around to say I was implicating her when I wasn't. I needed to set the record straight and reassure her that I did what I could to quash the lie that had been spreading about her. My mate's girlfriend was understandably worried that someone was out to ruin her reputation. It was all a lot of nonsense over nothing and typical Brighton gossip. Even so, she was upset as you know how fast rumours travel and stories get blown up. So, there I am on the call, standing in the middle of a little laneway just off Piccadilly Circus outside the offices my company rented (in fact they may not even have been paying any rent as they had no money) and as I look up, I see the familiar face of my old SVP (Senior Vice President) Peter from the company I'd left only a month or so before. He gestured to me and I heard him say, 'Hey Formula 1 Phil.' He continued as I finished up on the call: 'I heard what you did: brave move. I could really use someone like you on my next assignment. I'm off to Hong Kong.' He then reached into his pocket and scribbled down his email address on an old business card and mouthed, 'Call me, mate.' No sooner had he appeared, he was gone. We started communicating and a month or two later I had rented my flat out, sold my car, separated from my girlfriend and had my passport in my hand with a HK visa in it and was on my way clutching a one-way ticket. With only a couple of big bags packed, it was goodbye Heathrow, hello Hong Kong, for a two-year contract and the biggest pay-day of my life.

That, my readers, is serendipity right there. Or, as I am learning, maybe just maybe I am part of a bigger plan as the pieces for my life's puzzle start to reveal a clearer path. I was heading south, getting pulled closer and closer to the land Down Under.

As I edit these chapters, I do so with an influx of well wishes due to my current health situation from past and present friends and colleagues, and one thing that I am blown away by is a common thread of my decency and transparency. Many female school friends independently have gone out of their way to specifically remind me of my strong moral compass and that they always felt safe, respected and well regarded by me. Yes, these pages may make me out as someone who had become hardened, superficial, chasing the money but, as mentioned, I've always known right from wrong. Relevant to this story, it was important for me to step outside that day to make that call to my mate's girlfriend, to right a wrong that I was inadvertently drawn into – and look what unfolded.

CHAPTER 12

Hong Kong Philly

Hanna-Barbera/Warner Chappel – Theme to
Hong Kong Phooey (1974 onwards)

In this chapter I talk about the many cultural experiences that I
had, including the nuances of how business was done just that
bit differently, and culinary challenges. I also dive into the work
hard play hard culture. This sets the scene for me closing the
door on my life in England and opening new ones.

MY CAREER TOOK me all around the world as you would
have read in the previous chapters but it was my move to
Hong Kong (HK) that really super-charged my desire and ambition
to see as much of the world as possible. I remember very vividly
having a brief chat with Peter, who was the guy I introduced in the
previous chapter, where I spoke about serendipity. Peter and I were
just casually chatting in the office one day after I'd only been in HK
for a few weeks. He asked me how I was settling in and of course
it had been great, so I told him as much. He then responded with
some words I've never forgotten and were the best piece of advice
I've ever heard in my life:

'Once you have lived and worked in the Tropics, you'll never
work anywhere else again.'

The tropics of course being the Tropic of Capricorn, the region just below the equator, and the Tropic of Cancer, which is the region just above the equator. He was right. I've never wanted to live anywhere else in the world since. Although Australia where I call home now isn't strictly in the Tropics, it is not far from it. It is difficult to explain properly unless you know the feeling, but for me it's about the pace of life and the importance you place on the activities you do. Life becomes more focused on the outdoors for one and your spare time isn't so focused on the weather, a constant source of conversation if you are from that cold little wet island they call England. The constant need to chase the sun by having your summer holiday booked as soon as you get back from the previous one is removed. If there is a downside, then the closer you get to the equator the less you notice the changing of the seasons. Hong Kong had two seasons from what I could tell in the limited time I lived there – my contract was for two years – and I noticed it was either summer or typhoon or hurricane season depending on where you were. In East Asia this destructive weather pattern is called a typhoon, in other areas of the world they are called hurricanes. (This memoir is becoming more of a meteorological lesson than life events but every day is a school day, as they say). Oh, and it was humid at times – very humid. It also got dark at the same time pretty much every day, 365 days of the year. So, no lovely long summer evenings as you would experience in a northern European climate: it was dark by about 6.30pm most nights. I've always said since arriving in Sydney that I don't feel the need to go on holiday, as for me at least I feel I'm on holiday every day. Sydney for me has the perfect balance of life from a very mild winter through to blissfully gorgeous summers. Now that's enough about the weather but old habits die hard, I'm afraid ... Let's get back to the stories.

Where do I start with HK? So much to talk about. Since it became widely known I was writing a book, a lot of old friends have got in touch and said, don't forget the time this happened or that happened. All of them great of course, from the time I was marooned on Lamma Island (a small island near HK) where I had to leave a ferry operator my expensive watch to secure safe passage home or the event that widely became known as Phil the Ring, or a plethora of other amusing anecdotes that I'm not sure quite fit within the themes of this book.

Why don't I just start at the beginning and see where it flows?

When I first arrived in HK at the age of 29 I had already done a fair bit of travelling with work and visited just about every major city in Europe. My previous base was London: I worked out of a very glitzy office in the Piccadilly area predominantly and I later moved to live in West London after leaving Brighton when my relationship ended with Suz. So I was used to big cities and deep down inside I'm more of a city slicker than country bumpkin, so the draw of a heaving metropolis like HK acted like a big magnetic pull on me. However, I couldn't have prepared myself enough for what was on offer.

The sheer scale of the buildings, which if you've never experienced it before, is awe-inspiring. Sure, there are streets after streets of towering buildings in London, Paris, Düsseldorf, Vienna and others but it's the sounds and smells of HK which are quite unlike other cities. After all, one tall building looks very much like another when viewed from street level. It was this viewing from street level that caused me to have my first painful incident in the country.

You know in the movies when the lead character arrives in a new city and they walk around gasping in amazement at everything and everyone seems to be smiling at them and they are smiling right back. I was so intoxicated by what I was experiencing I totally negated to look in front as to where I was walking. My vision obstructed by what seemed like a million people, I walked straight into one of those bright red fire hydrants protruding from the pavement that connected firmly with my knee, so much so even a few people in the street went, 'Oooh owwww' as I buckled in pain. I didn't feel like Hong Kong Philly the Super Guy at that point and hobbled off down the street with my newly acquired injury.

My first brush with the local culture was an unexpected event where I had to visit a fortune teller or the Chinese equivalent, for my name to be translated into Mandarin for my business card. The Chinese place great importance on tradition and protocol. To hand over a business card with the local dialect and your name translated was of the utmost importance when initiating business dealings or discussions. Even the simple act of exchanging business cards was an intricate art form that, when done well, sees the relationship get off to a positive start. You hand your card over and accept the recipient's card by holding it between your two index fingers with their name face up, all the while maintaining eye contact and only breaking it to briefly look at their name and job title. Not sure if it is done the same way now with the proliferation of mobile phones but that is at least how I was taught to do it back then. Following this process will ensure good guanxi between both parties. Guanxi is a term used in Chinese culture to describe an individual's social network of mutually beneficial personal and business contacts. It cannot be underplayed and you ignored it at your peril! Anyway, it turns out that my name translated into Mandarin is Hoi Yee See which means Deep Thinker. Oh, the accuracy of that when I look back on it. At the time I didn't give it much thought at all, clearly not thinking deep back then, but how that changed. Or maybe it didn't change, I was just in too much of a hurry to register it then.

I learnt an invaluable aphorism in HK when dealing with the local culture and doing business, that stated that a Chinese person will only let you eat his catch after fishing with him for 80 years. They clearly understand Westerners' greed and will use this mercilessly to their advantage but they do not think in this way at all. They play the long game, which serves them very well.

I vividly remember one night when I was out in an area called Lan Kwai Fong or The Fong as it is locally known. I walked into a bar where I knew quite a few people. I worked the room, saying hello to everyone I knew, which was a standard process for me when I entered a social situation. One English guy I got to know quite well, who was a senior manager at a large recruitment company, stopped me as I was saying hi to people and said, 'Wow, you really are a player, aren't you Phil?' At the time I brushed it off but I didn't really care for the comment. Looking back, was this an example of East meets West? The Chinese call it guanxi and it is steeped in tradition whereas the West turn their nose up at it and call it a player. I will leave this one with you as to how you look at it.

Another common trait of mine was often finding myself the last one to leave. It would regularly get to a point in the night where there was no more point in the night or early morning for that matter. Later in life this trait would continue, much to the dismay of my then partner and now wife Melinda. She could not understand why I did not have an off button when it came to work Christmas parties for example, coming home at all hours in the morning despite being nearly 50 years of age. It was one of those bones of contention that we worked on. It was suggested that I become the chameleon in these situations, slipping on the suit that most suited those around me, so more and more people liked the outside of me, didn't feel challenged by me, and in turn I didn't have to show the real me.

Maybe it was this that the English guy was alluding to and that is what I took offence to.

Back to the stories ... As you can imagine, the cultural experiences were to become incredibly commonplace. Not least of which I was reminded of when talking about a particularly memorable culinary experience over dinner with my daughters and Melinda's parents recently – The Ten-Course Snake Dinner! My girls were asking me what the food was like in HK, what it tasted like and consisted of and I think by the end of this story they regretted the questions. It certainly brought back many memories retelling it all these many years later and with it fresh in my thoughts it seems like as good a time as any to tell it. It has a back story of course ...

When I first arrived in HK, I knew no one and whilst I've never been afraid of making new friends, the process of starting an entire social group from complete scratch required some new skills.

A quick insight into HK is that it is essentially made up of three core groups. They are colloquially known as ABCs, BBCs and CBCs. These abbreviations stand for American-Born Chinese, British-Born Chinese and finally Chinese-Born Chinese. They are all pretty self-explanatory. The fourth group, I guess, would be all the expats that lived there. I have no idea what the percentage of each make up of the 1.4 million inhabitants that cram onto the tiny island but I made myself familiar with the Canadian-Born Chinese that confusingly are also known as CBCs. When it came to somewhere to live, there were no real websites for house-sharing as it was still 2001 and so it was a simple case of just picking up the SCMH (*South China Morning Herald*) each morning and scanning the classifieds for rooms to let.

After just a few days of searching, I happened upon a suitable ad that was in the mid-levels area of the city which is home to the infamous Lan Kwai Fon or The Fong as mentioned earlier. It's a real party locale and many nights would start there. It was a lovely two-bedroom apartment upon inspection and Michelle, who was one of two sisters who lived there, explained that her sister Jennifer was moving out and a room had become available. We quickly hit it off and a date for moving in was agreed. What really sealed the deal with Michelle was when she asked if I smoked or not and I replied with, 'What do you mean by smoke?' I didn't know then that the Canadians were big pot-smokers! We both looked at each other and smirked. You could say at that point a friendship was born. My company had put me up in a hotel for the first month or so in a fairly humdrum part of the city called Shatin, which is most famous for its horse-racing course. The Chinese are huge gamblers, if you didn't know already. I was looking forward to moving in with Michelle but as the date approached she rang me with the news that Jen wasn't moving out after all.

I was gutted and she was too. As a means of showing her disappointment at how it had all worked out, she very generously offered to introduce me to her circle of friends as she was aware I was looking forward to expanding my social circle as well as finding somewhere to live. An offer of dinner at the flat was duly extended and I got to meet all her great friends consisting of couples and singles, both male and female. The food was superb and I later learnt that Michelle was a bit of a demon in the kitchen. My new-found friends however had plans for me. My diet growing up and well into my twenties was very simplistic and it would be fair to say I was a meat and two veg kinda guy at home. I loved eating out, don't get me wrong: like most people, I enjoyed experiencing new tastes and different foods, but nothing could have ever prepared me for The Ten-Course Snake Meal. I was told by Michelle and Tiffany – who was part of another couple that I became very good friends with – that it was a tradition to go to this amazing restaurant in Lok Fu and try snake.

I had already been alerted to the wide variety of animals on offer in HK. In fact, there's a joke that did the rounds: 'What's the only thing with four legs in China that doesn't get eaten at meal times? The table!!!' So, you could say I was kinda prepared.

I was already familiar with the delicacies of mud crab – at a certain time of the year they were a must-have feast. They were served boiled in a large stainless-steel pot and quite honestly, I had to force a smile as they were presented and I had to wrestle with the animal (it was dead, truth be told) to extract the minuscule amount of meat from the foul-smelling crustacean, in what felt like an experience that was taking me more energy to eat the food than it was to give me back. When Jim (another friend) asked me how I was finding my first mud-crab dinner I had no hesitation in telling him it seemed like an extraordinary amount of work for very little benefit. I had also already been subjected to a bone marrow extravaganza at Michelle's one evening where upon sitting down to dinner I was presented with a small spoon, very much like a tea spoon, but with an unfeasibly long handle. Naturally, I enquired what this type of spoon would be used for. Having no idea how the marrow was cooked or eaten and watching the other reactions of Tiff and Espen, Tiff's partner, it was clear I was in for a surprise. There were big cheers as a huge platter of food promptly arrived. Exquisitely presented of course, as was Michelle's forte. I can't remember exactly what was on the plate but it all looked fantastic and my anxiety went down a level or two. It soon went straight back up a few levels when my plate was placed in front of me and I looked down to see what at first glance appeared like some bones from an archaeological discovery where you may have then heard an archaeologist proclaim, 'Over here, I think I've found the tail!'

Espen, who was now grinning from ear to ear and looking straight at me, said in his Swedish accent, 'Hmm, looks good, doesn't it, Phil?' He of course was being sarcastic. Michelle looked at me and chimed in with, 'Tuck in, Phil.' I looked at her blankly and she grinned. I was beginning to get the sense everyone except me was enjoying this. No doubt they had been through this process with other unsuspecting diners as they had all their responses timed down to the second. Michelle instructed me to pick up the unfeasibly long-handled teaspoon, then pick up one of the bones that was about the size of a mini sausage roll and put it on a separate small plate next to me. I pushed at the long train of bones with the spoon, very much like a child who had just been presented with a seemingly inedible food for the first time. Though even as a child I don't recall being this puzzled or indeed terrified by a plate of food. As I stalled for time, the others were by now enthusiastically picking up pieces of bone with their hands and putting them on the aforementioned designated plate. The purpose of the spoon was then revealed. If you've ever eaten bone marrow you'll know the next bit, but having skillfully repositioned the smallest part of the bone chain (the very tail of the animal is the best for the finest-tasting marrow, I was told) in front of me, I was then told to dig around in the bone and scoop out a spoonful of marrow. The taste was not actually that offensive to my simple palate and I managed to finish off my portion, aided by copious amounts of wine and beer. Much like I did with the mud crab.

So, with mud crab and marrow now experienced in all their oriental delight I thought I was as ready as I'd ever be for a ten-course snake degustation. How wrong I was!

The restaurant was in an area of HK towards the north of the region, more widely known for its traditional culture. This was new to me as up to this point most, if not all, of my time had been spent on Hong Kong Island, which is differentiated by its more Westernised style of living.

Michelle, Tiff and Espen had all been to the restaurant before and led the way from the MTR stop (MTR stands for Mass Transit Railway and is the equivalent of the London Tube, New York City Subway or Paris Métro) at Lok Fu.

Once inside it didn't take long for me to notice the very basic set up of the tables, which only had a simple plastic tablecloth covering the surface and I was struck by how different it was to the more luxurious surroundings of the restaurants on Hong Kong Island that I was used to. The waiter and Michelle spoke to each other in a very quick exchange as was quite normal for locals and I just listened, not knowing what was said in the slightest. I also noticed there were no other Westerners dining and everyone eyed me quizzically as this young gweilo man looked around apprehensively. Gweilo is the name given by locals to most white-skinned people and is literally a translation of ghost man. It is not generally considered a compliment and could be used by locals as a derogatory way of addressing you. At its worst it's like the term 'negro' or worse such words starting with N. As we sat at the table that was being prepared for the meal Michelle had ordered, I noticed one wall in the restaurant was just a floor-to-ceiling arrangement of small drawers, about the size of a desk drawer. Rows upon rows of them. Whilst not your everyday sight in a restaurant, I had seen a lot of strange things since arriving in HK and wasn't overly distracted by it. By now we were all getting hungry and the waiter took no time in asking us more details about what we were having. Michelle did her machine-gun-fire verbal exchange with the waiter, at which point he looked over at me and smiled with a big grin. I sensed something was brewing.

A few minutes later, the purpose of the wall of drawers was revealed in all its glory. Or I should say all its gory glory!

We all looked at the waiter as he went and opened one of the drawers that was at about shoulder height. In one hand he had a pair of tongs very similar to a set of BBQ ones. He slowly opened it – at which point I was greeted with a sight I will never forget. A bunch of writhing snake heads all appeared with their tongues out, tasting the air and struggling to break free from their drawer-shaped enclosure. The waiter skillfully deployed his tongs to capture one of the recalcitrant invertebrates and, once firmly in the tongs' grip, it was pulled free of the nest of the other slithery occupants. The snake was about 24 inches long and I had no idea what type it was other than it was soon to be a dead one. It would die the most shocking death imaginable. As it writhed and wriggled, the waiter somehow got it on its back and held it whilst he produced a small implement not dissimilar to a surgeon's scalpel. With one hand he rubbed the belly of the snake in one continuous motion and direction, appearing to feel for something and upon finding it flipped the snake towards a small bowl that had been placed nearby. He then used the scalpel to make a small incision in the snake's belly, at which point some indescribable contents oozed forth from the slit made by the knife. I was in a state of disbelief by now and desperate to know what the hell was going on. I looked at Michelle, who nonchalantly informed me I was about to try snake bile. The waiter looked at me as he squeezed the area around the incision and a small sack about the size of a small grape popped out of the snake. He looked at me and without the slightest hesitation he very proudly told me, 'Snake bile, good for the virility, sir – old Chinese tradition.' I was appalled at what I had just witnessed but the worst was yet to come. The small bowl was then filled with some liquid that smelled like the type of pure alcohol you find in a school chemistry lab. The small sack, which appeared to be still attached by a thin membrane or similar body part, was cut free with the knife and washed in the bowl of liquid which presumably was used to sterilise the toxic fluids present in a snake's belly. Once cleaned, the sack was sliced open with the scalpel and some kind of luminous green fluid oozed forth and flowed into the bowl of alcohol, but separated in the way that oil and water repel each other. Once all the fluid was in the bowl, it was stirred which had the effect of turning the whole contents of the bowl green. The snake by this point had just been unceremoniously dumped back in the drawer, so if I was feeling a bit queasy I had to spare a thought for the poor snake and all the others dotted around in the numerous drawers waiting to be turned into dinner whilst dealing with the loss of a vital body part.

The waiter presented the bowl of putrid green fluid to me, which I was told had to be drunk. There were cheers from the assembled diners as they knew this part of the routine – there was no way to back out of it, so I just gritted my teeth and glugged it all back in a single go. Well, what was it like? Like a mix of brake fluid, pure alcohol, petrol and a big dose of relief once it was done – disgusting!

For what seemed like an eternity, course after course of snake arrived. Soup with snake, deep-fried snakeskin, snake on a bed of bok choy. Then, thankfully, there was a break in proceedings for my stomach and a large ceramic pot was placed in the middle of the table and I was told we were now having chicken. Thank goodness for that. Luckily or unluckily in this instance I've always been good with chopsticks and so had no problem helping myself to the contents of the pot. As I was digging around in the pot, my chopsticks found a hard lump at the bottom and since the contents were obscured by an oily residue on the surface of the soupy meal I had no idea what I was trying to pick up. I persevered and finally, after a few minutes of groping around in the oily broth with my chopsticks and now with a firm purchase on the object, I triumphantly announced I had picked it up ... whatever *it* was.

As I looked at it, a sense of dread came over me again. You know how when you are shown a picture and at first glance you have a hard time making out what you are looking at but the more you concentrate the more the image is revealed. This wasn't some kind of optical illusion but a real-life game of guess the body part and animal. As I stared at the blackened object, it came to me: I was in actual fact looking at a boiled chicken skull. Though I didn't exactly know it was from a chicken but I could tell it was a skull of some now deceased animal. What alerted me to the fact it was a chicken's skull was Espen rejoicing, 'He's got the chicken skull!' with great fanfare. I was a lucky man by all accounts and all the other diners thought the same too, if their reaction was anything to go on. In complete contrast I personally thought myself the most unlucky person in the world at this point.

Exactly what I was supposed to do with this body part was a mystery to me but I assumed whatever it was it was likely to have something to do with my virility. It seemed most hideous foods were sold to Westerners on the pretext of improved virility and I certainly wasn't particularly concerned about being deficient in that part of my life. It turned out I was to put the blackened skull in my mouth and crunch down hard on it; this would crack it open at which point I was to break it wide open and eat the brain straight from the skull with my chopsticks. Now the whole restaurant was looking at me. I really felt I had no choice. Talk about group pressure. I took a deep breath, put it in my mouth as instructed, bit hard, heard the crack, quickly spat it out and somehow removed the brain and did the dirty deed. Cheers erupted all around the restaurant and I felt a strange sense of accomplishment that I had achieved something that really should not have made me feel good but it did and I was glad it was all over. How was my virility, I'm sure you want to know? As expected, no change at all. What did the snake taste like? It tasted like chicken, funnily enough. Now I had completed my full trifecta of strange animal meals, I retreated to the comfort of BBQ duck and pork for the rest of my time in HK.

I've spoken a lot about the social side of my time in HK but there was a serious element to my stay there and that was my work. As you have no doubt gleaned, I've always had a really good work ethic as far back as I can recall; however, this attitude was seriously tested each and every work day and you could say I finally learnt the meaning of the saying 'work hard, play hard!'

During my time in London things got pretty loose on a regular basis. It wasn't just me but the whole of the group that I surrounded myself with. I only highlight this because even with this sort of behaviour I always ensured I maintained a good work output throughout and HK was no different. However, it brought a whole new meaning to the 'play hard' half of that saying, which meant to balance this you had to work even harder.

I remember buying myself some crucial corporate brownie points at work one day. It was after repeated delays of us receiving our telecommunications licence from the HK government, which would enable us to sell and operate our services. Remember about the Chinese playing the long game? Well, they certainly set out to delay us. This one day, Peter the CEO witnessed me in full sales mode trying to get a deal over the line that was crucial as he had a very important board meeting coming up where he had to show progress in our commercial activities. My reseller account that I was in charge of had a deal but was very slow in closing it out (the long game again). In my frustration, I bellowed down the line, 'Am I going to get the deal or not?' and promptly slammed the phone down. I sat back in my chair, sighed and rolled my eyes only to turn around and see Peter in the doorway, arms crossed and looking at me. I paused nervously before greeting him but before I said anything, out came from him, 'Atta boy Phil, I knew there was a reason I employed you!' I always got on well with Peter. I told him that the deal would be in by close of business Friday. It was now 4pm Friday. Later that afternoon, before we broke for the weekend, I joined Peter for a beer, watching the various street entertainment that was going on just outside the office. He asked how the deal was coming on. I assured him that it would be going ahead. He disappeared back into the office and I watched nervously as the lift doors closed but it wasn't too long before he reappeared, clutching a signed A4 faxed piece of paper heralding our first cross-border sale for our new telecommunication network. Someone in China had just signed over their company's profits to our company in HK due to our superior product. Peter and I exchanged glances – I nodded my head and knew my work for this week was done.

This story would have relevance for much later in my life when I made the switch from corporate to build my career in the high-end design industry and found myself in a relatively senior interview for a sales manager position. Basically, high-end design and the products were certainly exclusive – but humdrum bathroom furniture and fittings? I was asked by the company owner how I was going to make taps desirable and sexy so that my sales team could sell them. I recounted the above story, emphasising that if I could make telecommunications attractive then I could do the same with the company's products. He put his fingers together and looked across the table at me and said, 'Wow, you really did sell rice to the Chinese?' I had a little chuckle to myself, agreeing I suppose I did; I had never heard it being put quite like that before. I was ultimately offered that position but declined as I had accepted another one elsewhere. When I was going through that interview process, the head of the company exclaimed, 'You really do have the gift of the gab!' Seems my granny was right all along.

Back to HK and I thoroughly enjoyed my time there but, in the end, did not see out my two-year contract as the Chinese doubled down in their efforts to stall our entry into the market. This meant that work slowed as we couldn't launch our products despite our early success. I was offered a number of special projects that I ultimately declined to take up. They say every man has his price and by now, I had my burgeoning bank account and an offer from some old Brighton mates to join them in their world travels to Canada, America and South America. True to the introduction of this chapter, I would never work again in Europe. I was off to travel the world and then take up residency in Australia. I'll see you in Colombia!

CHAPTER 13

Colombia

Oasis – Columbia (1994)

This chapter, which quite honestly could fill a whole book, is just a snapshot of mine and my mates' time in Colombia, South America, which forms part of our much wider adventures and travels 'on the gringo trail'. It also formed what could have been called my gap year – starting in Whistler snowboarding for a season, then to the States and on to South America with a group of lads from home after my stint in HK and my last hurrah before settling in the land Down Under.

MUCH OF IT is unprintable! Suffice to say there were many nights of nonsense. Actually, that's not strictly true. I don't want to give the impression all we did most nights was get loose. I said at the start of the book I wouldn't deliberately mislead the reader, so in the interest of a balanced perspective of our time travelling it must be said there were many days packed with nonsense too!!!

Colombia is a country that is most commonly and widely known for one thing. I'm sure I don't even have to spell it out here and now. As tourists, and in this case my travel buddies and friends of friends etc., you mostly only get to experience one side of the country and the all-important culture of drinking (mainly rum or ron as it's known in most places) – which me and my travel buddies would regularly refer to as 'Two rons not making a right' while we refilled our glasses! This is great of course and an incredible never-to-be-missed experience but alongside all the big nights out, there is a really sad world of exploitation and danger that exists in a lot of South American countries that cannot be overlooked. (At the time I overlooked it every day of course and couldn't wait till sundown to get back ron it!!!) Essential reading whilst travelling in this area was *Marching Powder* by Rusty Young. A very worthwhile read, giving a very detailed insight into the other world that exists in South America. I won't go into the politics of life there as this is covered very accurately in Rusty's book – so much so I recently bought a copy for my father-in-law as we were chatting about my time travelling the world when working on the book.

For this chapter, I'll stay away from the hedonistic activity that filled most days and keep it as clean as possible. This book is supposed to be a family show and besides, the tale of misadventure that I relate to you and makes up this chapter is just as readable.

The story starts innocently enough with a bit of sightseeing. We had been holed up in our hostel for a few days, only really venturing out for food and essentials. Probably best not to imagine what those essentials are made up of in a place like Colombia!

In most South American towns and cities, on top of the highest point in that town or city there will be for religious reasons a large statue of Jesus Christ. Most commonly he will be displayed with his most observed pose of arms out in front and a 'big fish' width apart. Just have a look at the world-famous statue at the top of Mount Corcovado in Rio to see what I mean.

It was time to venture out of the hostel and first on the list of places to see was old JC telling us his big fish story just up the hill nearby.

Dressed in only our jeans and lightweight clothes, we started our ascent along a dusty old track that led to where we wanted to go. It was mid-morning but already the heat of the day was starting to burn down on us and it wasn't very long at all before we had drunk our pathetic supply of water that would only have kept a baby pigeon's thirst quenched and were now looking for somewhere to rest up. After a few hundred more yards, a perfect spot presented itself in the form of a rickety old bench at the edge of the dusty track. Sitting there, we surveyed the view around us: it was magnificent with all the flora and fauna and the wide array of colourful rooftops of the houses and buildings of Cali, the town we were staying in. Whilst Pablo (Paul's nickname for the entire trip) and I were sitting there, both our sights landed on the small opening to what appeared to be a cave entrance. There was no sign carved into the rock face indicating as much but as any bloke will tell you, a guy knows a cave when he sees one. Maybe it dates back to our predecessors' era when shelter meant survival and that part of the brain is still hardwired or maybe it was because we were just stupid little kids deep down inside but we both simultaneously saw the opportunity for some adventure – not that we needed the stimulation as the trip offered already more than enough of that.

The cave had a small opening, was dark inside and looked for all intents and purposes exactly like your typical cave. If you had asked a small child to draw a cave, this is how it would have looked. We took no time in deciding we should set about becoming cave men for the morning, and what a mistake that turned out to be. If you are at all squeamish, then probably best to skip forward to the next chapter. As soon as we had both ducked through the entrance with Pablo leading the way, it instantly became clear it was quite a few degrees colder in the cave and dark. No lighting like you see in images of mine sites with bulbs festooned along the walls and ceiling. The floor was now damp underfoot and the smell of mossy rock was starting to fill our nostrils. By now we had ventured all of 10 metres in our cave exploration and were unable to see anything with any real clarity. Pablo dug the small disposable lighter he had on him out of the pocket of his shorts to illuminate what was up ahead and we inched forward step by step. After a very short period of time the lighter started to burn his hand, so we foolishly decided to carry on in the pitch blackness of the cave. After a few more stumbled footsteps and deciding the lighter had cooled enough, he flicked it back on and immediately stopped dead in his tracks. Only able to make out a gloomy outline of Pablo a step or two in front, I bumped into him and with the lighter now only giving a flickering flame I saw the look in his eyes that I knew, along with the words: 'Run, there's a monster!' Knowing Paul for many years and knowing he didn't scare easily, this meant only one thing ... Yup, you guessed it ... Run, there's a monster!

I turned and made like crazy paving and got cracking. I've always been a fast runner and this occasion was certainly no different. Pablo is a little shorter than my 5′10 and due to the height of the cave I had to bend down a bit to clear the ceiling. I could hear the pitter patter of his footsteps right behind me but still no sign of the monster. I could see the entrance to the cave by the light just up ahead. Now if you've ever tried to run in the bent-over position you'll know it's not easy and, driven by the thrill of reaching the cave entrance, I went into full sprint mode, fully extended my stride and went full speed in the direction of the light up ahead. I probably got less than five metres when something very painful happened.

Suddenly a feeling that I can only describe as being hit over the head with a club hammer occurred.

My head stopped immediately but my legs still in full Road Runner cartoon-mode kept going. I went horizontal for a brief moment, then fell slap down onto the cave floor. Due to the poor light, Pablo could not have possibly seen what took place and despite the noises I was making carried on running. Obviously fearful the monster was out to get him, he kept going towards the light. In order to get to the light of the entrance he had to step over me or, more accurately, tread all over me. So, as I lay there with my head ringing and little canaries circling over my head just like in the cartoons, he proceeded to first stand on my throat, neck and chest and then, as he carried on forward, step on my groin before finding the solid ground of the cave floor next.

Some time later – I'm not sure exactly how long I was motionless on the floor for – I regained my senses and having now forgotten all about the monster (if there ever was one), I scrambled to my feet and using both sides of the cave for coordination and support I got myself into the standing position and took a few moments to take stock of the situation. As soon as I got vertical that all too obvious metallic taste of blood was in my mouth. I had not been attacked by the monster so all in all, things could have been worse. I'm not sure exactly how but I was at least still alive I reasoned and took some comfort in that fact.

As I blindly emerged from the cave, the midday sun made focusing on anything very hard. This, along with the ringing in my head, meant that basic functions of thought and concentration were all but impossible. Gradually my vision cleared and I made my way over to where Pablo was standing. The look on his face was not one of encouragement and he turned away from me very quickly. As I stood there in the midday sun with my head hanging forward,

I noticed blood dripping onto the dusty ground at my feet. I immediately saw it wasn't the sort of blood you get from a cut or scratch, from a cat's claw or shaving injury; no, it was that dark red, thick gloopy type that more resembles the makeup you use on Halloween. I instinctively knew I had to stem the bleeding and using the shirt I had tucked into the waistband of my shorts I twirled it into the type of shape you would normally use on a tea towel if you planned to towel whip someone. I reasoned the blood was likely to be pouring from my forehead so this bandanna-type makeshift medical device was the most appropriate, I thought, with my very limited roadside medical knowledge. I began to wrap the emergency material round my head, all the time very concerned my favourite French Connection short-sleeve shirt was getting ruined by all the blood. It was simply one of those shirts that I loved. It fitted great, was ideal lightweight material for the climate but as of now its stint as a favourite white shirt was over and it was time to take one for the team. Just as I was bringing the shirt into position Pablo, who hadn't said much since leaving the cave and was for the most part just standing there with a look of horror on his face, said, 'No, Hillsy! As you raise the shirt up, try and do it from below as you've got quite a large flap of skin hanging from your head and you need to somehow get it back into position.'

Armed with these basic instructions from a non-professional medical person and having very little else to go on, I duly followed his advice. Now with the blood flow stemmed, the priority was to get back to civilisation. We'd come about the laughable distance of one kilometre from the hostel we'd set out from for our morning walk. A two-year-old child could have walked further, unsupervised and quite honestly with fewer injuries. We now desperately needed to get back to safety. Whilst heading back down the route we'd taken to get up and with more to concern ourselves with than yet another view of the big fish story-telling JC, we embarked on our descent.

We passed several similarly motivated sightseers who were heading up to where we had planned to get to and instead of the customary head nod and hola there, attention in us was a little more intense. One group asked if there was anything they could do to help and was I in fact okay? OK being a relative term and considering I'd just left most of my forehead and the bridge of my nose – oh yes, maybe I haven't made it clear but my face was a total dog's breakfast – on the cave roof and was now bleeding profusely. I guess I probably wasn't in the grand scheme of things 'okay'.

One guy who spoke good English stopped for a chat and upon realising we hadn't been attacked and mugged, which wasn't unheard of for tourists in this part of the world, told us the quickest way back to the hostel was in fact not down the track but down a steep part of the hillside. Armed with this invaluable newfound knowledge of the area, we acted quickly and without even questioning it or the validity of a complete stranger's instructions, we started scrambling down the hillside. I was now starting to feel quite dizzy, which may have been from the heat or the concussion or the blood loss, or quite likely all three.

After what seemed like an eternity, we saw the welcome sight of the small white building that was the hostel and went in to get help. There were gasps from the ladies running the place and they immediately started to offer their assistance in every which way. One grabbed my shirt and replaced it with a wet tea towel and as she did so I told her to be careful as the sight was pretty full on and the blood had started to dry and the loose skin had now stuck to the shirt. Fortunately, their English was very good so we explained there had been a case of misadventure and no one else was involved. I think Pablo joked you should see the state of the other bloke. One of the hostel staff said that a trip to the hospital would be best so Pablo and I jumped into the hostel owner's car and proceeded to Cali hospital with my favourite white shirt soaking in a bucket of bleach.

The next few hours are a bit of a blur, if I'm honest, but I do remember a couple of things. Laying back on a hospital bed and having a large hospital container of some kind of fluid poured over my forehead. I never did know what that was. May have been a hospital beaker of ron for all I knew. It certainly felt like it as it stung like hell. But I suspect it was some kind of sterilising fluid to clean out the wounds.

The other event I clearly remember was digging around in my pocket for my wallet and handing it to Pablo, telling him there was a gold credit card in there and to get me fixed up whatever the cost. A little while later and after Pablo had disappeared with clear instructions he reappeared, looking all pleased with himself whilst simultaneously announcing to me that he did in fact have some good news. The last few hours had been particularly scarce on anything good to mention, other than we hadn't in fact been eaten by that pesky monster that started this whole sorry story off. So eager to get the good news out of him, I encouraged him to share more with me. At least it wasn't one of those occasions where someone gives you an unenviable choice and says to you, 'Do you want the good news or the bad news?' I'm sure you can all relate to a time when someone has given you that choice, one that does little to buoy your confidence in what you are about to be told.

If you go to the pictures section of the book, you will see whether it was money well spent.

In fact, someone later told me that due to the high number of violent crimes and attacks in the region, the hospital staff's skills on a medical level are actually first-rate.

Unbelievably, I left the hospital that same afternoon. There were no scans and very soon I was back at the hostel with the only problem being that my face and head had swollen up into a shape which, according to my mates, was changing every hour along with bruising that was starting to become more and more obvious but for the most part resembled the look of a character called Manimal who was popular on UK TV many years ago. He was half-man, half-beast, so it was by no means a comforting lookalike. As the hours and days wore on, my mates would laugh when they looked at me as my face continued to change shape and colour.

To this day I still have a scar across my forehead and on my nose. The one on my forehead for some time was not too dissimilar to Harry Potter's jagged feature. Look that one up as well, if you're not already familiar with this distinguishing mark of his.

We hung around in Cali for a little while longer, so if there were any issues I could get them looked at but in the end the stitches were removed without issue and I made a full recovery. They actually injected silicon into my head to build up the area so when the skin was sewn it didn't leave a noticeable dent where the flesh of my forehead had once been. The only scare came a few weeks later when I absentmindedly headed a football before the area was fully healed and the skin split a bit and some strange fluid oozed out. It was no more than a small talking point that had otherwise now been forgotten about, except when I felt like winding up Pablo over a bottle or three of rum about the monster he apparently saw.

Had I learnt a lesson from the accident other than don't believe Pablo if he says he has seen a monster and that we should run for it? In fact, this brings me to a point. I've heard it said that memoir writing is not just about being able to recall events accurately but also tell a story through the art of storytelling. I would also offer that providing a meaning in said story is just as important. This brings me back to the title of the book. What was I trying to prove? That in fact I went to Colombia and drank my own body weight in rum every night along with the consumption of other unmentionables. My life was on the face of it just one big ego trip and I was just as much into proving things to myself as I was proving things to others it would seem. How long would it be before I realised this?

The only major road block to this was staying out of danger long enough to learn this valuable lesson. The problem was that each of these stories would end in another incredible tale worthy of gathering an audience around me and reciting it, thereby fuelling the ego evermore. One thing for certain after this big event was that I was reminded of the song lyrics of being much happier with a bottle in front of me than giving myself a frontal lobotomy.

I mentioned earlier that there is no real way of knowing the day your life will change forever without the benefit of the 20:20 vision of hindsight, and let me tell you from my own personal experience of my cancer diagnosis, you never see it coming. So, for now at least it would appear this potential life-changing moment, along with many of the other stories in this book, would just be chalked down as another great story to be told whilst all the grandchildren gathered around and sat on Grandad's knee in the lounge in front of the fire. Once again, another opportunity to change went begging.

I've always considered myself a fatalist in that all our lives are preordained to a lesser or greater extent. Yes, sure, you make changes as you go through life: it's called free will. But just as when a magician asks you to pick a card and even if you change your mind at the last minute to fool him, it doesn't matter as the cards are already stacked for or against you, life, I feel, has the same outcome. It knows when you will make a sudden sharp turn and has that already factored in. That isn't to say you can just tear around being as reckless and irresponsible as you like, knowing that the path is already laid out. You still need to take responsibility for your life by being present and listening to what presents. Call them 'stop moments', if you like. You would probably have guessed by now that I ran a few stop signs, figuratively speaking.

I've already introduced the idea of the feather duster, the brick and the bus moments in our lives. Well, this was a brick moment I brushed off. How many more bricks would I face? And was the bus just around the corner!?

PART FOUR

MOVING OVER TO DOWN UNDER

Seeking out life in paradise which, at the time, I thought was going to be the final piece of the jigsaw.

CHAPTER 14

Better Than a Miracle

Chvrches – Miracle (2021)

As referred to earlier, my only brush with the Australian medical system was when both my daughters needed specialist care in the first year of their lives. In this chapter I describe what went on for them and how this affected my relationship with their mother. Of course, these weren't simply miracles but very well-orchestrated medical interventions that I could only marvel at.

WHEN I WAS around the age of 37, my partner Lauren and I decided to start a family. Lauren was about 32 at the time, I seem to recall, and her female body clock was ticking. A lot of couples in our circle who were a few years older were heading down that route already. Being a father wasn't something that immediately appealed to me. If I looked into my crystal ball and projected one, five or even 10 years ahead I imagined many things in my life, but children were not one of them. However, it was a big thing for Lauren as she had recently lost her brother very close to his 18th birthday in an incredibly tragic car accident involving a drunk driver. Max was a fantastic lad who I got on really well with. I swiftly did a U-turn in my attitude as I felt it was time to give something back to the cosmos. Max had been to Australia a year or so before to visit Lauren and me when we were living in our inner-city pad in Crown Street, Woolloomooloo. Sue, their mum, was also out and we had a great time. I had decided that although marriage wasn't a pressing matter for me at the time, the decent thing to do was to propose to Lauren and have a long engagement. Since Lauren's father had passed away just recently, again in tragic circumstances, I would ask Max on his trip out if I could marry his sister. Of course, you would normally ask the father but since that wasn't possible, I considered it an honourable thing to do and get young Max involved.

I told him of my plans for his sister whilst he was here on his trip with his mum and he was delighted. I explained we would go around all the high-end jewellers in Sydney and spend a decent amount and choose an engagement ring for his sister. I asked him what the most amount of money he had ever seen was and whatever his answer was I explained it was going to be a bit more than that we would be spending that day whilst getting treated like royalty in places like Cartier, Bvlgari, Chanel and Tiffany's, plus a few others.

We spent an awesome day shopping around, being shown some beautiful rings and offered drinks and nibbles everywhere we went. The experience was pretty special, I can tell you. I did have a budget but having just finished a very lucrative two-year contract in Hong Kong it was pretty substantial.

After a day of hiking around we settled on the classic four-prong Tiffany engagement ring with a decent cut and clarity stone and a carat size that didn't shout, 'Hey, look at this massive rock my partner just bought me!'

In fact, I could have got one twice the size for half the money, made exactly the same by a private jeweller who was prepared to throw a very, very nice Oris watch into the deal. I am a tragic watch freak, so the deal was extremely tempting but I stuck to my guns as I knew the classic Tiffany box and ring would blow Lauren away when I knelt in front of her and presented it.

Max and I left the city feeling very pleased with ourselves and I'm sure if he were still alive he would remember that day very clearly. We all headed off to Byron Bay a few days after, where I proposed according to plan.

Although the contract in HK had been very lucrative, the money pot at the end of the rainbow wasn't an endless stream. Having just started my own business, which as any small business owner will tell you runs into the many tens of thousands, along with the costs involved in us both becoming Australian citizens had put a big dent in my war chest. I knew that after I had proposed the obvious next step of children were to follow and we needed to consider costs like maternity leave to cover as the Australian system back then was hopeless, to put it mildly. In fact, we were dealt a really cruel blow when we went to get all the Centrelink admin sorted out and were denied payments as we hadn't been citizens for the pre-requisite 104 weeks.

We had done our transition from lowly 457 Working Visa holders to Australian citizens in the least amount of time possible, but it still wasn't fast enough.

I'm a classic car tragic and had bought myself a very nice Triumph Stag when we first arrived in Sydney. Lauren wasn't a huge fan of driving and so having a classic car as our main mode of transport wasn't a problem. However, it was time to buy a second car for us with children now on the way. I've always been a big fan of 3 Series BMWs so I bought us a very nice second-hand one as the family car. But again, it was another expense I had to fund, as I rarely if ever buy things on finance. I always fund things through cash.

I feel a bit bad for putting Lauren through this ultimatum, but a year or so earlier I had basically said out of children, marriage and home you can choose any two of the three but I can't afford all three. Lauren had her heart set on having children, and because we were already engaged, the marriage, we decided, could sit on the back burner for now. Perhaps settle on a long engagement. A very long one it turned out to be and it never made it to marriage, but I'll come to that later.

For some unknown reason I was adamant my first born would not be brought back to a rented apartment, which most expats lived in at the time. Fortunately, Lauren agreed, so kids and home it was. In a strange twist of fate, the GFC had just crashed down on the world and the immediate knee-jerk reaction was for a lot of property investors to unload assets. We were lucky to cash in on the crisis and secure ourselves a charming, large Art Deco apartment in a lovely suburb called Randwick. Neither of us had lived there before but it had wonderful amenities like a great high street with an all-important mall, a racecourse that the apartment was on a hill behind, good transport links and an even more important children's and women's hospital that, at the time we weren't to know, was going to play a very significant part in the first few years of both our daughters' lives.

Part of my rationale behind ensuring we were owner occupiers when Scarlett was born was so that we could, or really I should say 'I', could fully decorate her nursery in our choice of colours rather than the limitations of a rented place.

Time was running out between Lauren's due date and the settlement date, so I had to get a wriggle on if I wanted to get the whole apartment renovated in time for her birth. The numerous scans that are required on the lead up to the birth showed Scarlett was underweight and there was a good chance she would need to be induced on or around the due date, so there wasn't a moment to lose.

The flat was one of nine in an old Art Deco block that had wonderful large rooms, high ceilings and a lot of original features like cornices and mouldings. Unfortunately, there were a lot of other original features like the kitchen and bathroom. Lauren wasn't too impressed from the outset as we were currently living in a fantastic city apartment overlooking the Opera House, Hyde Park and the Harbour Bridge. It had floor-to-ceiling windows all round, a fantastic swimming pool and a concierge.

I knew however that the place we were buying represented great value for money and I told Lauren to trust me that when I was finished with it, it would be ideal. I set about hastily renovating the entire apartment on my own. We were fortunate that the whole block was owned by one person prior and was now being sold off as nine individual apartments, which meant there was no one else living there as all the flats were sold with vacant possession and we were the first to buy and then move in. Which was just as well as I was up to all hours banging around getting the place fixed up. I did a bit of a cheeky move as normally there is a six-week period between exchange of contracts and settlement and it's only then you can get the keys. However, on one of our previous visits I had left the kitchen window unlocked and once we exchanged, I was straight round there with a couple of paint pots and a few tools. My recent career flip to industrial design, where I'd started my own design studio and that I'll talk about in an upcoming chapter, meant I now had a fully equipped workshop and was able to undertake a large number of joinery tasks required to do the kitchen myself. It was long hours though and I'd leave home around 7am to be at the studio for 7.30 to 8am for a day's work, then head over to the flat around 5ish with all the things I needed for that night's tasks, finish up around 10 or 11pm and then rinse and repeat for the next four weeks straight. I enjoyed doing it and I had painted, carpeted, laid hardwood floors and renovated the kitchen by the time we settled, which meant we moved into a fully finished apartment. None of the hard work was for nothing as four weeks later Lauren's waters broke. It gave us a chance to move in, get settled and have everything ready for when we brought Scarlett home after a relatively straightforward birth – well, straightforward for me anyway as I wasn't doing any of the pushing. It wasn't long before the problems began, however.

After a day or two of bed rest and loving our beautiful but small baby Scarlett, we were all but ready to leave the hospital when the doctor did his rounds. He was about to announce to Lauren she was all clear to leave when he used his stethoscope and said Scarlett had a double beat on her heart, or a murmur, and would need to be checked further. We were devastated of course and over the next few days it transpired she had a hole in her heart or VSD, as it is clinically known. Lauren would always say she was born with a broken heart as the reason we brought our starting a family plans forward was due to Lauren's brother being killed a year or so earlier. Anyway, we were allowed to leave quite soon afterwards and told to come back and see the specialist or go to A&E if Scarlett developed shortness of breath or trouble breathing. Holes in the heart are actually very common and there are thousands of people roaming the planet who have them and don't even know. The soonest they find out is, when say, an unfit 40-year-old man is playing football one day and suddenly croaks it.

I learnt during my crash course in cardiothoracic surgery and talking to the specialists that the hole can either be in the muscle or the membrane part of the heart. One gets bigger as the heart gets larger and the other tends to close up as the heart grows. I can't remember exactly which is which but as luck wouldn't have it

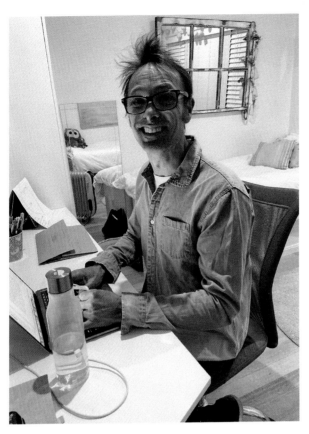

Nearly one year on from landing my dream job as area manager for Australia and NZ for a global acoustics company, I was home from hospital (the first time) starting my book. Note my humble office – the girls' room where I had made their beds and desk not long before starting.

Running amok in Colombia
2003 with the lads; me after
coming off second best in a cave
with a monster.

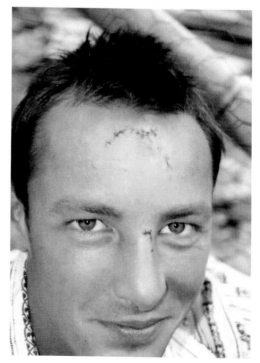

My love of cars: starting out early with my sister Maria circa 1973; my Lotus Evante – my last car when I was in England and it was going to be my retirement project, now sold to a lovely chap in the UK who is already showing it in car shows – with the girls on a trip back to the UK in 2013 and then again in 2018 for a work trip; teaching Scarlett to drive early in the family silver BMW E36 circa 2012; The Range – another project that was cut short but I loved her while I owned her! And finally The Blue Baby – 1999 Convertible E36 – I made sure she went to a very good home.

What do they say about cars? 'Love your cars and they will love you back', 'You don't choose your cars, they choose you', and the one that has helped me the most in letting go: 'You are only ever a custodian of your car.'

Starting out Studio Maizon, first in my mate's garage and then in my own studio on Crown Street, Darlinghurst, Sydney. Appearing on ABC *New Inventors* and my signature round coffee table and rolling pin lamp made it into *Belle* magazine and *Australian Home Beautiful*!

My 50th in hospital where I first sat in a wheelchair to go to radiation (previously I'd be wheeled down in the bed), then celebrating with the girls that night. Coming home. And venturing out again with my crazy hair-do – including our engagement dinner.

Marrying Melinda, 26 March 2022.

Our 'Celebration while I
am still alive' event, end
of April 23, where Melinda
read a eulogy of sorts with
me adding my two bobs
worth from time to time,
our good friends Rachel
and Lucy said a few words,
including reading the
last chapter of my book,
and Lyla said her piece.
Otherworldly, divine,
stunning, gorgeous day
for all!

The last two years of my life have been nearly as full as my first 50 combined! Included here are pictures at our home together and our family moon to Port Macquarie with Mum and Dad, and where we hooked up with Julie and family.

Scarlett had the one that pointed to it growing larger as the heart grew, which almost certainly meant heart surgery. These types of problems are called congenital heart disorders and operations to fix them are pretty routine but even so, opening a baby and performing heart surgery is obviously best avoided where possible. Scarlett was still very small for her age and small babies are not as strong as bigger babies, so the decision was made to get her weight up before performing open heart surgery. Incredibly, if detected during pregnancy, this operation can be carried out in utero.

Lots of trips to and from the specialist were required and luckily, as I mentioned earlier, we were only a short walk from the children's hospital.

Each visit, the story was the same: wait for her to grow a little bit, then we will operate. Scarlett didn't seem to be in any distress, so we were happy to go along with the advice.

Eventually the day came though and we were going to have to get ready to set a date for the operation, so one last scan was performed. The specialist started to get really annoyed with his scanning machine, bashing and cursing it. Eventually, his assistant wheeled in a new one. Scarlett, only four months old, was doing her usual thrashing around, making all sorts of commotion. I have to say it was quite a stressful environment to be in. Anyway, eventually a new scanner was found and the specialist got on with looking for the hole – but to his absolute astonishment it was nowhere to be found. Literally a medical miracle had occurred, and the upshot was he told us to go home and enjoy our daughter as no more visits were required. The stress levels immediately subsided, and I don't think I have ever been so relieved in my entire life. Certainly beat the feeling of selling those RSL shares that time.

However, the story doesn't end there. Due to their small size it's quite common for underweight babies to not be good sleepers as they can't take in enough milk or food to sustain them for long periods of time. Scarlett was one such example. To add to matters, when they sent the placenta off to the lab as they do with a lot of babies with issues (very small in this case, the size of a borderline premature baby not a full-term one), it turned out she had what they call a velamentous attachment of the umbilical cord. There are a number of reasons why this is significant. For one, the risk of the baby dying whilst in utero and during birth itself is significantly higher. Basically, instead of the umbilical cord attaching to the correct part of the amniotic sac, it attaches to an area that's much thicker and harder for all the blood and nutrients to get through to the baby – hence her small size. They literally have to fight to get their nutrients to stay alive. So, Scarlett came out fighting from the very start and boy, did we know it.

Scarlett joining the world with these medical complications at birth (she's all good now) meant she was very restless for many years. We tried Karitane and Tresillian sleep schools, but she beat the system ... nothing worked. Later, when she was big enough, co-sleeping with me was the only way she would fall asleep, even when our newborn Lyla arrived nearly three years later. Early on we knew it was dangerous to sleep with small babies. So, one night I thought, I'll finish this once and for all ... I would do the controlled crying bit and I would not cave.

Anyway, every time I patted her and she was slowly drifting off, I would try and walk away but she would start screaming again.

This went on for hours ... 12am ... 1am ... 3am ... 4am ... 5am ... 6am and then sunrise. I'd been awake all night and my arm was sore from leaning over the side of the cot ... then at 7am Scarlett sat bolt upright and gestured that she was hungry ... so we had breakfast and went off to day-care ... She was happy as Larry. Mind you, if Larry had been living next door, he wouldn't have been very happy I can tell you. Neither Scarlett nor I had slept a wink all night. That was a tough day's work.

It still haunts me to this day, and I don't think I've ever fully recovered.

In the end I co-slept with her for about another three years, so we could all get some peace and quiet.

Phil 0, Scarlett 1.

Moral of the story: sometimes you just gotta let the kids win :)

In fact, even to this day some 10 years later when Mel and I are in bed just drifting off to sleep, I'll start rubbing her head in the pre-conditioned way that I did for so many years with Scarlett. It's a mannerism that's been drummed into me.

Now then on to Lyla, my second born nearly three years later. This time a much more relaxed pregnancy so I am told; obviously had nothing to do with me apart from the very beginning. There were none of the problems of before whilst leaving the hospital and we returned home after a few days with our beautiful Lyla. The flat was great as it had two large bedrooms and a smaller sunroom that doubled up perfectly as a nursery. It was part of the reason I pushed us so hard into securing the apartment. I knew from the outset it would serve us well into the future. In fact, Lauren still lives there with the girls to this day. I expected it to last five years but to see it still going strong after 12 is just fantastic. Nowadays they don't build them like they used to.

Unfortunately, problems with Lyla were only just around the corner and it was me that first saw them.

As was customary back then, I would bathe with both girls before bedtime. The apartment had one of those super big old-style tubs that you could fit a rugby team in if required. So, it was more than suitable for me and two small girls come bathing time. I had done the routine many times before and tilted Lyla's head back to get the soap off her head as she had a bit of cradle cap that needed attending to. However, when I brought her head back upright, she had this glazed look in her eyes. I can't tell you exactly what I saw but it scared the bejesus out of me. So much so that Lauren, who was in the bathroom, saw the look on my face and knowing that I wasn't the type to scare easily, asked immediately what was up.

I can't remember my exact reply to be honest, but I think I mentioned something about her appearing to just stare into the distance with a faraway look for a while. We were used to babies constantly wriggling around and not keeping still for even a few secs, so it caused alarm bells to ring. We got her off to bed okay that night but when I got home from work later Lauren said she had seen Lyla do something very odd with the pack of cotton wool balls whilst lying on her change mat. She had picked them up and started shaking them overhead.

We were both alerted by this behaviour but not overly alarmed as those jerky movements when babies are young are very common. Anyway, the next day Lauren was at the park doing the standard-issue maternity-leave trip round the neighbourhood and stopped to talk to another mum, when this other lady stopped Lauren mid-sentence and said words to the effect of: 'Is your baby alright?' When Lauren looked down, there in the mountain buggy was Lyla, having what to the untrained eye was an epileptic fit.

She soon calmed down; Lyla, that is. Lauren's and my nerves were on edge for years to come – and when I got home that night and was told, we decided to go to the hospital. There was not much they could do and as the episodes had passed, they told Lauren a handy trick which was to put the iPhone into video mode on the front screen and if it happened again to video it.

Sure enough, it happened again but I'm not sure if Lauren was quick enough to capture it. Anyway, she did manage to capture one very soon after so we went straight back to the hospital and showed them. Whilst we were waiting for a team of specialists to review the video, Lyla had another episode right there in front of them. I can tell you from first-hand experience, there is nothing more heartbreaking than watching your daughter have an epileptic seizure in front of you and being told to keep away from her until it passes. The reason is that the muscles in seizure mode are strong enough even in babies to actually break bones if you try to stop them. Well, at least now we had a specialist confirm the diagnosis and we were promptly admitted to the hospital. Lyla would have been no older than six months, if I recall correctly.

They dosed her up on some anti-convulsant intravenously to fast-track getting her up to therapeutic levels of phenobarbital. The episodes came under control and it was time to start that horrendous period of hurry and wait for all the tests to be done to identify the cause.

Lauren stayed with Lyla that night whilst I went home and obviously, though I'm not proud to say it, started googling away on what it might be. The really nasty one is a condition called West's Syndrome and I'm not even going to go into symptoms and prognosis here, but it's not pretty.

The next few days were a bit of a blur and consisted of a lot of specialists coming and going, but one of the few things that does stick in my mind was Lyla just sitting or lying in her hospital cot, totally oblivious to the commotion going on around her. Meanwhile, being in a such a specialist ward there were other mothers and fathers all dealing with their own horror story, wanting to talk to anyone who might be in a similar situation and needing reassurance to ease their obvious pain. It was a really, really tough few days and when I left one night when visiting hours ended, I actually stopped by the little chapel they have in hospitals and prayed for the first time in my life. It was quite a defining moment and one I will never, ever forget. If you've never prayed before, which I hadn't, it's actually really hard to know what to say. So, I think I knelt, put my hands in the tried-and-tested position and blurted out a few unrehearsed words.

Finally, Lyla was booked into having an EEG test, which involves wearing a cap with electrodes on it that measures brain activity.

We were very lucky to live so near the hospital and I could just walk up every day with no dramas about parking or having to factor in journey time. The GFC was still having an effect and my business was only just regaining traction and getting back to activity levels pre-GFC, so being self-employed I was able to literally down tools and head to the hospital as required.

The level of care in the Randwick Children's Hospital was outstanding until one day a registrar came to see us after the EEG had been done and we were waiting for the results. We were standing by the cot with Lyla just sucking on a dummy or playing with a toy of some description and the registrar walked over to see us. I'm not sure who said it first, Lauren or me, but it was basically, 'What did you find out?' He then replied, 'There was some very suspicious data on the EEG.'

Well, that was it for me. I nearly passed out on the spot. I felt my legs weaken under me and had to hold on to the side of the cot to stop myself from going down. Lauren burst into floods of tears. It was a horrific situation. Luckily, at that exact moment Professor Anne Bye, who had been assigned to oversee Lyla and incidentally is the top paediatric neurologist in the country – how fortunate were we that she happened to have her clinic at the Children's Hospital – walked past and came over to see what the commotion was about. We told her what just happened and she rather unreassuringly told Lauren and me to follow her into somewhere more private. Well, if I wasn't already on the edge of sanity this was enough for me to nearly throw up on the walk to a small room, just off to the side of the ward.

Once we were all in the room, she asked us to take a seat, which I refused to do as I was too revved up. So, I just blurted out, 'Has she got West's Syndrome?' I said this uncontrollably through a dry mouth that was, I swear, holding back a stomach full of vomit. Prof Bye looked at me in astonishment. 'No,' came her immediate reply. 'Why do you ask that?' I stammered that the registrar said they had found some very suspicious data on the EEG. 'Oh that,' Prof Bye said. 'It was just that one of the electrodes wasn't connected properly.' I've never felt so relieved, even more relieved than when the specialist said Scarlett didn't have a hole in her heart and the time I sold my RSL shares. I can tell you both those occasions belong in the hall of fame of relieving events in my life.

'So,' I went on to ask, 'What is it and will Lyla be okay?' In a manner of complete composure, which I guess you would have expected from a professor, she said, 'We know the least about the brain compared to all the other organs. Only Lyla will give us the answers.'

It was a great reply and summed it up perfectly. Lyla went on to make a full recovery over the next nine months. Although we did have one scare. It's important that the anti-seizure medication is kept at therapeutic levels. Lyla had blood tests every week to check this. The phenobarbital was administered twice a day by syringe with a liquid inside. Trying to make a 12-month-old child stay still while delivering this foul-tasting liquid each day was hard, to say the least. She had been seizure-free for over three months which, even on medication, was a good sign. Then, one day, she started to have seizures again, so we rushed her into hospital with the fear of God in us. They ran some tests and found the levels of the drug were so low it was barely working. Little by little, all that spillage out the side of her mouth night after night had reduced the medication so it was barely having an effect. They dosed her up and the seizures came under control; at about 18 months they gradually weaned her off and she's remained seizure-free ever since. Seems the Prof was right: Lyla really did have the answers and they were the right ones.

Of course, as with any great story or stories of survival and triumph over adversity, unfortunately there are the victims as a counterweight. In this case it was Lauren's and my relationship. It's funny, you know; you often hear about how couples are brought closer together following a harrowing set of circumstances but yet others can go the other way. In fact, I can tell you, Mel and I have taken this time since my diagnosis to really deepen our relationship and see the quality in what we have together.

Lauren and I never got to that point and as life continued to press on, even with two now healthy children, our relationship just rattled on and seemed to slowly die. Of course, tokenistic efforts were made to rekindle the love and intimacy we had before these events, but they seemed from my side to be just that, tokens. Nothing substantial or long-lasting.

The ongoing GFC was putting pressure on not just us but everyone. We had done very well to 'cash in on the crisis' with the property purchase and I knew I would never put myself in any form of financial peril – I'm confident if you've learnt anything so far about me from this book, it's my attitude to money. Lauren, who had now had one year's maternity leave, was getting worried my stash was dwindling fast, especially with rising interest rates post-GFC. She would say things like, 'What are you going to do when it runs out?' I was of course under a lot of sustained and heavy pressure, but I found her attitude quite tiring all the same and did my best to put her mind at rest. I tried to explain that I still had a six-figure sum to draw on and there was no need to worry. My business, then only in its second year, was still ratcheting up and the GFC had affected it but actually not too badly as it turned out. After we had children, I soon started to realise that being an expat had its downsides and a major drawback was lack of support. When you go through all that we had to endure without the shoulder of parents or the wider family to share the load, life becomes very tough. Very tough indeed. I've never been close to my family. We weren't close when I was young and as soon as I was old enough and had my first proper girlfriend, I wasted no time whatsoever in moving out. In fact, when I moved out, I didn't even think to tell my parents. Apparently, the evening after I'd stuffed a few of my belongings into whatever old English sportscar I was driving at the time, when Dad asked at some point where I was, Mum responded with, 'Oh, he's gone.'

I've never been the type of person to 'live under my mum's skirt' I think the expression goes and so my independent ways were ideal as an expat. I lived in Hong Kong for nearly two years and I could count on one hand that's been involved in an industrial accident – which it has and more on that story later too – the times I spoke to them. There certainly wasn't talk of them coming out to see me or really any phone calls I can remember off the top of my head.

Juggling the constant competing demands of sick children – coughs and colds as well as congenital heart-type illnesses that play havoc with day-care and your ability to work – should not for one tiny moment be underestimated when you can't just pick up the phone and rally the troops.

I would be lying if I said there wasn't any family help; however, it was somewhat of a mixed blessing. When I met Lauren many years earlier I got on really well with her mum and when she visited, we had an amazing time. But as soon as Scarlett was born, her attitude towards me changed and she turned on me faster than the weather in Tasmania. Having visited the island many times to see Mel's family, I can tell you nothing changes faster than that.

All of a sudden we went from having great times together to me being public enemy numero uno. I simply didn't understand what I had done wrong. And that was just the point, anything that I did from then on in was never enough, not good enough or just plain wrong when it came to looking after my daughter. Why was it that my fathering ability was coming into question when prior to this my abilities were never questioned? I loved looking after my daughter and there was nothing I would do to put her at risk. The bond between us is unbreakable.

Parenting is innate but there are practicalities that I would defer to Lauren about like how do you know when the water is warm enough for bathing our new born that found me being pounced upon by her mother. There were many examples and if you've ever had children, you'll know how tired you are in the first year and proceeding ones and I was bone-tired and mentally as well physically exhausted and just lost the plot with the continuing undermining comments that were raining down on me. I could have handled things better in hindsight but after all that I had done to make her daughter's life as easy as possible, it was too much to bear. What was even harder to bear was that Lauren did not step in to defend me. I thought you had each other's back in relationships and I was clearly out on a limb in this trying time. To say this played havoc with our already weakening relationship is an understatement.

The relationship with Sue continued to deteriorate, which was all the more disappointing as we used to get on so well. Sue used to come over for months at a time and although the flat was big, doing musical beds to fit her in was an unnecessary logistical challenge that we could have done without. The continued barbs directed at me and with close living conditions, the situation became untenable. So, while I wished for some family support, as the old saying goes: 'Be careful what you wish for.'

Fast forward a handful of years and life was about as good as it had been for some time, and was going to be for many years to come. Lauren, who plainly knew the fractured relationship I had with her mother, boldly announced her mum was coming for the summer and staying with us again.

I knew this was going to be the proverbial straw to break the camel's back and went into survival mode.

The already well-withered stump of affection that was called The Lauren and Phil Show was not capable of sustaining this sort of pressure. I knew the guy I had been sharing the workshop space with had a spare room, so I checked if it was still available, which thankfully it was. I explained to Lauren my decision and promptly left that night with absolutely no objection to my departure.

I'm not sure if I was expecting her to throw herself across the doorway to block my impending exit, but it never happened of course and I was dismayed that Lauren had chosen her mum over me. When I met Lauren, what I saw was that all she and her mum did was argue and I felt sorry for Lauren. In the time we had been together, Lauren's life had changed immeasurably, having gone from living in a rented room in a council flat just on the outskirts of Brighton and a job in a call centre with no real prospects, to living in one of the most beautiful cities and countries in the world, of which we were both now citizens. She had a flourishing career in corporate Australia, living in an affluent suburb, not just when we arrived in the city but later in the apartment in Randwick. She now had a driving licence at the age of 30 and two beautiful daughters. In fact, I had made having a licence a precondition of having the kids, as there was just no way you can ferry yourself and kids around without one. All these things I had a major instrumental part in orchestrating and making happen. I just couldn't fathom what I had done wrong to be treated so badly by her and her mother. Lauren clearly knew our relationship was in its death throes, but instead of looking at ways to keep us together, she decided to throw all her efforts into pleasing her mother when she knew full well this would place serious pressure on us. As I recall it, Lauren's words to me were, 'So I've finally driven you away?' or something to that effect. The reality was as I fired up the V8 I was driving myself away. If you want a job done, do it yourself. I was very used to doing that. Let's just say I left and never at any moment looked back. I left with a bag packed in my Range Rover* and wondered why I had put so much on the line over the years, but I guess it just goes to show you never really know someone after all.

---

* I neglected to introduce my beautiful 1994 Range Rover – I flew over to Adelaide (South Australia) to buy it when the girls were young with the view that it would be great for when we went camping. There were a number of families that we used to do this with each year and the girls still go with these people. But also, for me to be able to take the girls down to the snow each year. I loved the snow and wanted to share it with my girls. Remember, I started my year-long travels with a season in Whistler. I drove the Range back the 1400km interstate, all day and well into the evening. I remember getting to Dubbo, a five to six-hour drive away, thinking, 'Great, I'm nearly home' but in reality, there still being quite the drive ahead. On arriving home Lauren was not overjoyed by my purchase exclaiming 'Over my dead body are you taking the girls anywhere in that!' As mentioned, she had lost her brother in a car accident and so for her driving experiences were now tainted. Me on the other hand knew I would never endanger my children's lives and again couldn't understand the lack of trust. We were clearly growing apart.

At the time, I did a trade with my spanner man to do the necessary maintenance on this lovely old machine: he got my Stag and then did the work on the Range for free when needed. Unfortunately, as my life weaved its twists and turns I never did get to the snow in it but much to Melinda's surprise the old gal went up in value in the time I had it and I was able to sell it for nearly double what I paid for it. Classic cars, you have to love them.

CHAPTER 15

⎯⎯ ❧ ⎯⎯

Making the Break

Bronski Beat – Smalltown Boy (1981)

You leave with almost all your clothes in an old suitcase
Alone in your car it's a tough and lonely drive to your new place.
Adapted from original lyrics from this song.

Here I introduce a character called James who is a fellow
designer/maker and who helped me out when I was in need.
I also give you background as to how Maizon started and a
few of the BIG mistakes I made.

ALTHOUGH IN THE last chapter I said I never looked back, that wasn't strictly true, if I'm honest. As any father, or any parent for that matter, will tell you, saying goodbye to your children, whether it be dropping them at school or in this case leaving the family home, is one of the hardest decisions you'll ever have to make in your life. I devised a way to continue to see them whilst simultaneously ensuring Scarlett, who was about five, but not so much Lyla, as she was still very young, maybe two or so, weren't aware that I had left. This involved leaving the place I had moved to at around 7am, driving from Balmain back to Randwick, letting

165

myself in and being there by the time the girls woke up around 7.30am and also allowing Lauren to get ready and head off to work without having to do the time-consuming task of the day-care or school run. I got breakfast ready for them, got them dressed and would take them both the short distance by foot and pushchair for Lyla to day-care and then Scarlett's school. My job allowed a more flexible start time as I had just started back with an old work colleague, James, who luckily was more of an owl than a lark. After all the drop-offs were complete, I would walk back to the flat, jump in my car and head over to Leichhardt where James had his workshop. I finished at James's about 5ish and would then do the run back to Randwick to pick Scarlett up from school or after-school club and we would both nip across to Lyla's day-care. Scarlett used to attend there when she was younger, so the day-care teachers were over the moon to see her all grown up. We would take a stroll through the park and get back to the flat where I would fix up dinner for us all, bathe the girls and have them ready for bed by the time Lauren got back from the city. It was then just the simple matter of doing bedtime stories, which we did together. Once they were both asleep I would head off back to James's and then repeat the same thing for the whole week. This continued for quite a while as it gave Lauren and I some much-needed space away from each other whilst allowing the household rhythm to continue. Sure, it was a bit of faff doing all the running around, but it was a neat transition arrangement and a doorway to the next stage; we got used to our new lives apart from each other while keeping an all-important watchful eye on the family unit. I can't actually remember what we did for weekends, but it would have involved me making the trip back east and being there for a few hours each day to include either waking up or going to sleep time at a minimum.

This continued for many months, maybe even a year or so – I honestly couldn't say – then one day I decided to break the news to Scarlett when I picked her up from after-school club. I told her that I was still going to be very much involved in her life as I was at present, so nothing would really change. Scarlett took it really well. Yes, there were a few tears, but we were really tight and she trusted me, so one way or another we got through it. Lyla was still too young to realise fully what was happening.

Now is a great time to properly introduce someone who became a large part of my life and who I met around 2009. James was the gatekeeper to The Castle. Just so I'm not misleading the readers in any way, it has to be explained that the name 'The Castle' is an ironic nickname. Much like you might call a tall friend 'shorty' or a bald friend 'curly'. The castle was for the most part a dilapidated run-down weatherboard cottage in Balmain. It had plants growing through its walls. The plants could get through the walls due to the big holes in them. He had a spare double room, and the rent was very reasonable given the condition of the house. James often rented out the spare room and my timing could not have been more perfect. He was also a fellow artiste/industrial designer/furniture maker. I didn't come through the conventional design route to become an industrial designer, so as a consequence of this, I did not have an established network of people with similar backgrounds. Therefore, it was quite natural for me to conclude I was very much alone in my endeavours but in actual fact there I was, staring at an almost carbon copy of myself. Even our age and birthdays were spookily similar. I became quite close to him over the next decade or so as we forged a creative business partnership that would have us working on many joint projects, including café fit-outs and various high-end apartment renovations, along with unique furniture designs.

We had very similar skill sets that were uncommon in people of our age and backgrounds.

When I had my design studio in Darlinghurst, it was positioned in a very good spot, located near the corner of a busy junction of Crown Street and Oxford Street. The studio was easy to spot and in a vibrant locale. There were also a lot of pop-up stores in the area, which is where James fits in. One day a larger-than-life character wandered in as if he owned the place. A character trait I quite like actually, as I have often been accused of this very action in the past. He began nosing around. Over the years of dealing with customers, you naturally develop an extra sense of their intentions. My studio was half workshop, half retail store. It was the ideal combination for a business like mine that relied on my skills to make the furniture and also be on deck to liaise with customers and discuss their requirements, without having to employ an extra person to deal with the foot-fall traffic that entered the studio. Besides, being a salesman myself I was best placed to be front of house. Maizon was also still in its start-up phase and I didn't want to hamstring the business with extra headcount. People would go on about borrowing money to expand the business to allow for additional staff, but my financials needed to be good for three years to borrow money and given I had plenty of money saved from my corporate career before I did the flip to industrial design, I just wasn't comfortable knowing I was taking on extra liability when things like having children and buying a family home were just around the corner.

Back to James. He's a tall guy, at least 6 feet tall, swathes of unkempt locks and a good physique with scars and tell-tale skin blemishes of a man who clearly worked hard – and though it took me a while to find out, he played pretty hard too. He took a keen interest in my designs and clearly knew what he was talking about. He asked all the right questions about the fabrication of the pieces

I had on display and I knew immediately he was 'in the trade', so to speak.

I showed him the workshop at the back of the shop and he was quite taken in how I was able to produce all the things I did in the space I had allocated. The workshop, which I designed and built myself, had all the tools and machinery you could ask for. Cross-cut saw, table saw, thicknesser, pillar drill, bandsaw, metal folder, wood store and two large work benches, all efficiently packaged in a room that was previously the kitchen of the shop. A cat would have had a heart attack if it saw it as there was certainly no room to swing one. Every single square metre, or more accurately millimetre, was designed to be a productive space. Tools slid in and out of spaces that shouldn't by the laws of physics have even existed. But somehow it all worked, and it was my sanctuary where I spent the hours and hours required to make the magic happen. These were joyful moments. Australia is not generally considered a cold or wet climate but being sub-tropical it can experience some quite heavy wet weather events. Oddly, these downpours were some of my favourite times in the studio. The workshop was warm and dry, there were often no customers in the shop at these times and being cocooned away in my sanctuary was a chance to catch up on odd jobs, knowing that little else was possible while Sydney went through these soon-to-pass weather events. It has to be mentioned it wasn't always like this, however. Just the simple matter of having a waterproof workshop I couldn't take for granted. And my first introduction to not having a watertight workshop came very early on.

Let me rewind the tape a bit so you can see how making the transition to being self-employed evolved. At around the age of 35 and having been in Australia for about three years a realisation dawned on me. Despite living in a beautiful country with a great job and social circle, I knew deep down inside things still weren't harmonious with me. I just couldn't put my finger on it straight away but after a short time I came to the conclusion that it was my work that was unfulfilling.

Yeah sure, the money was great and the culture was appealing to me. Beautiful offices right in the heart of the city, only a short commute from home with on-site parking. Lots of co-workers my age with similar interests and so on. I did, however, find the prospect of spending the rest of some of my most productive years ahead of me as a middle-management spreadsheet jockey somewhat uninspiring. One of the things that has been a constant in my life for as long as I can remember is my restless inventiveness: whether it's tinkering with my cars or coming up with ways to modify or improve things, clothes, bikes, you name it. Even in my bedroom at home as a 12-year-old, I put a mezzanine level in, pulled the carpet up and wallpapered the room without running it by my parents. At one stage I even found some big old orange lounge curtain in the attic that I used to separate my room into half bedroom area, half lounge/office desk (that I built myself, too) to make it resemble a studio apartment. A mate and I would spend hours in the nearby big box hardware store, Wickes, I think it was called, working out how we would get large pieces of wood and mirrors home on our bikes and doing the costings of materials ... We had to stay in budget! Past life as a builder, anyone?

I had developed a very large social group during my first few years of being in Sydney. A combination of friends of friends, ex-work colleagues and a handful of others that you invariably meet through being an expat.

Once I had decided my career in telecoms was no longer filling me with a sense of purpose, I started to look for ways to bring that purpose back.

As mentioned, one of the constants throughout my whole life and certainly as long as I can remember has been the undeniable feeling of being drawn to the pursuit of the design of things. So, you could say it was a fait accompli that my choice of vocation would now be a furniture designer. Having been in Sydney a few years, I had moved a few times and as a result needed extra furniture. However, instead of wanting to go and purchase it, like most ordinary people in my situation would do, I felt compelled to make it. It started with a long bench for my hi-fi and TV, then rapidly followed by a side console table, that then gave way to a dining table and before I knew what was happening there were beds and chaise lounges and lights filling the flat. Much to the bemusement of friends and most definitely my partner, Lauren.

It was as if an external unstoppable alien or previous life force had taken over my body. My brain couldn't stop thinking about what I could create next and it felt like a lifetime of unrealised potential was uncontrollably unleashed in one go. It's fair to say I had found my renewed sense of purpose.

It's an old saying but a relevant one and one I will repeat again by the end of this book: 'Find something you love doing and never work another day in your life.'

I very quickly realised that Australia had an enormous supply of wood in many different species that I'd never come across before, which lent themselves to making the type of furniture I was interested in designing and making, namely thick, chunky hardwoods that created designs and pieces that were very of the moment, especially here in Sydney. Whilst doing my fabrication of the pieces I wanted to make, another thing started to become very apparent – the cost of these materials was really very low. Particularly when you compared it to the retail price a lot of shops were charging. I just couldn't see how some of the shops got from what the cost of the raw materials would be to the final retail price. I was determined that I could do similar for a lot less. I'd had various stillborn business ideas in the past, mostly around making objects – things like steering wheels for my car as I'm a total classic car nutjob and even a rolling machine that would make the art of rolling a joint a much simpler process than the ones on offer when I was around 20 or so. Yup, no prizes for guessing that I spent a bit of time in the stoner zone as a youngster. Me and my mates never went anywhere without a joint.

I weighed up all the pros and cons. On the plus side I had the funds following the lucrative stint in HK, plus I was young enough to make the switch, had the pre-requisite passion and knew there was a market for the product. All I needed to solve was the issue of where to operate from, as doing this kind of business from home (the flat) was not really an option. I did, however, take it as far as I could by building pieces on my large balcony and turning my storage cage that most Australian blocks of flats are allocated with into a wood store. Once word spread of my crazy antics and my network started to realise I was serious about this pursuit of becoming a furniture designer/maker, the customers started to materialise.

One such couple were Skye and Mark. Unfortunately, Mark is no longer with us due to dying of oesophageal cancer. But I have a lot to thank Mark for, as during a discussion about making a bespoke (which all my pieces were) shelving unit we got on to the topic of a workspace I needed to make all these bonkers creations and completely out of the blue he offered up his garage that wasn't being used other than for storage of random junk. It was at this exact moment you could say that Maizon was born. I had already come up with the business name and engaged a graphic designer to create my logo but this was the final piece of the jigsaw. Maison with an S is obviously French for house/home but all my pieces were going to be very contemporary and individual-looking, with the use of lots of interesting angles, which is where the Z in Maizon comes into play. So the tagline was to be 'Furniture for the home with a new angle to it'.

A bit cringeworthy looking back, but it kept my design ethos intact and ensured I stayed true to the original idea. I even designed a light called the Z light that was a signature piece of mine and always provided a talking point to clients. Coming from a sales background virtually my whole career I knew that 'images do the telling but stories do the selling'.

I needed no time in taking up this offer, a nominal weekly rent was negotiated and I took off with my ears pinned back at 100 miles an hour to make the garage my new workshop and base to work from. Upon investigation it was even more perfect than I had imagined. Rear lane access meant I was able to load and unload materials and had somewhere to leave the car all day. Which was no mean feat in Bondi Junction.

It was a single-car brick-built garage with a working roller shutter, good power supply and head room. I was over the moon. Mark owned the house, so there were no issues with leases expiring. The only other thing I had to do was to make the final leap of faith to giving up the day job. I needn't have worried as completely out of the blue I was offered encouragement by my boss. I can't remember the exact course of events or dialogue, but it loosely went something like this ...

At every available opportunity I would be sketching out ideas of designs, solving problems for designs I'd already been commissioned to make or doing some maths for costings for the business. My boss walked past my desk and saw me frantically scribbling away. He was a fellow English guy and we got on well. In an around about way

I told him I was starting to build pieces of furniture in my spare time for some friends and that I was naturally pretty good at this kind of stuff. Quite out of the blue, he replied that he used to be a CDT teacher before he got into sales. CDT, or Craft, Design and Technology, is a subject taught in British schools. It was available at my school but I had selected Engineering Metalwork as my practical option. Same, same but similar. He showed more than a passing interest in my thoughts and ideas – then told me why not pursue it further if that's what span my wheels, so to speak.

He was undoubtably more than a little surprised when I handed in my resignation at the end of the month. It wasn't quite as simple as I'm making it sound. I had a lot of moving parts in my life in Sydney that needed attending to. In the background of starting up the company, there were some immovable feats that needed moving. Most importantly my work visa. I won't bore you with the nuts and bolts of the Australian immigration system but essentially mine and Lauren's right to live and work in Australia was a direct result of me getting what is known as a 457 visa. I had got this visa through the Holiday Working visa route that in turn I had applied for before I left HK. It allowed your partner to work with unrestricted rights in any job they wished but as the primary visa holder I was tied to the company that had agreed to sponsor me. Most companies would sponsor you, but it meant they had an invisible bond that tied you at the hip and restricted your movements.

The only solutions were to get residency, which we were going to do but it was some years away due to application and statutory qualification periods, or get Lauren's company to sponsor her and me become de facto on hers. Lauren worked for a recruitment company at the time, but they were not set up as preferred suppliers of the visa class we needed. It was not impossible for them to become approved for this, it just took time and willingness from the company. Fortunately, they wanted to become an approved visa provider anyway, as it would make it easier to hire staff for themselves and the companies they were recruiting for. Box ticked. From memory we did have to pay for our visa but given the freedom it would provide, this was but a small price to pay.

So, with all the paperwork now in order, a prefunded business idea in place, a space to operate from, customers lined up, this was it! Time to back myself and put my money where my mouth was. I'm pretty sure I actually made a piece of furniture for the boss of the business to prove his co-operation wasn't in vain.

In the brief period of double-handling my job in IT and Maizon, I would make regular visits to the wood yard to buy materials for these jobs that were starting to pile up as word spread further of my newfound career path. The guys at the timber yard found it hilarious when I roared into the loading dock in my Triumph Stag with the roof down – it was the only way I could fit all the wood in – then jumped out still wearing my tailor-made Savile Row suit and Thomas pink double-cuff shirt, and started rifling through their timber rack, cross-referencing my checklist and hand-sketched designs for the lengths of timber I required. Looking back, it was outright bonkers but I was 30-odd years old and felt bulletproof. Out of sheer bewilderment, the guys at the timber yard cut and helped prepare the timber I requested and no sooner had I arrived I was steaming off, either back to the flat or workshop to turn my haul of raw materials into finished products. It was a steep learning curve but I've never been one to shy away from hard work or risk and this felt like such fun.

I once turned up to tennis, which I played every week with my mates, with stacks of two-metre lengths of wood in the car. A mate asked what on earth was I going to do with that lot, to which I replied: 'Make a four-poster bed.' I did and I still have it to this very day. (An amazing twist is that without it, I wouldn't have been as independent as I am with the disability I acquired as a result of the brain cancer – I use it as a rigid point of stability as I am walking in the bedroom – and it has stopped me going overboard on numerous occasions. In fact, we couldn't have done without it. Mel and I marvel at this regularly!)

As previously mentioned, it wasn't always fun on a number of fronts and the first issue was the part about having a watertight workshop. I had left work by now and was fully embedded in my life as a furniture maker. I had a commission from some old work colleagues who all lived together in a big house. They were looking for a dining table, but they knew my style was to accommodate the weird and wonderful into my work. Being self-taught, I wasn't constrained by the traditional way of doing things so I was prepared to give anything a go and the crazier, the better. They were a bunch of guys I knew from my corporate days who, like all of us, knew how to party. So it should come as no surprise to learn the bespoke request was to have a stainless-steel insert over a metre long down the centre in the middle of the table. No prizes for guessing why. I set about creating the design and making it in the workshop. I was nearly finished and very pleased with the result when disaster struck.

I had been out that afternoon and upon opening up the roller door I was confronted with a totally sodden and saturated work-shop. It had yaffed down all afternoon, which was the first time it had really rained since getting fully set up in the workshop and, unbeknown to me, it leaked – badly! All the walls were dripping with water, tools soaked but, more important than that, the dining table was awash with water all over it. I had no idea what to do. This wasn't in the manual. The sun soon came out, as it always does in Sydney, but the damage had been done. Over the course of the next few hours, small dark dots started appearing like a tropical rash – not that I've had a tropical rash, mind you! – all over the timber. I knew that the timber was a hardwood but not all hardwoods have the same properties. The hardwood on your outdoor deck is meant to get wet but the Vic Ash I had selected for the table ... err, not so much. Did I mention something about a steep learning curve? There is a great saying in woodworking that I committed to memory from the moment I heard it and that is: 'Keep your wood as long as you can for as long as you can.' Added to that one should also be: 'Oil your wood before you wet your wood!'

I was gutted and took the table apart as quickly as I could, but in truth I had no idea how to fix it, other than to leave it in the sun. Leaving things in the sun seems to work as an old wives' tale to remove stains from clothes, so why not wood? Surprise, surprise, it didn't work and the clock was ticking to get it delivered. Tick-tock ...

I designed all my pieces to flat pack so I could actually deliver them on my own and fit them in the Stag for ease of delivery, so I disassembled the table in the workshop and took it down to see my new friend Blake at the timber yard. He worked the huge panel saw they had there as well as a plethora of other woodworking tools. He was a great fountain of knowledge who took a shine to the work I was doing as I think it gave a bit of interest to his day. That is, instead of the tedious process of cutting up uninspiring MDF panels for hours on end.

I explained what happened and he knew. Basically, the wood contained tannins and when unprotected wood gets wet or very damp they are drawn to the surface and leach out. Tannins are wood's way of protecting itself from infestations and bacteria. They oxidise when the wood gets wet and essentially I guess the wood had gone rusty. Well, that's my schoolboy interpretation of what happened. Who'd have thought I would make a table out of wood that rusts! What a groundbreaker I was.

Blake suggested now the wood was dry we pass the timber through the thicknesser and take a few millimetres off one face of the timber. This should remove the black tannins (same as tea) that had risen to the surface. It worked a charm, but the only challenge now was that when I put the table back together, because the timber was a few millimetres thinner than it was designed to be, none of the planks lined up properly. The cost of getting all the timber machined again and remade meant that was out of the question as I'd charged mate's rates in the first place. I ended up delivering and installing the table on time but with a complete redesign that worked well, but the guys were a little surprised to see something very different to what they were expecting. I don't think they ever did pay me for it, even though they got their stainless-steel insert that I'm sure got well used. It's such a shame the iPhone didn't exist back then and a lot of photos of my early creations were never captured and are now just in my memory. I had a camera, but it had a memory card that would fill up then get lost before I downloaded it to the computer.

I often wonder where the many creations that had my hand in them are now. As a quick side story, I did have a very pleasant surprise a few years ago when I visited a second-hand furniture store and there, in the middle of the shop, was an old dining table I had made for a client in Woollahra. It was one of my typically creative designs in that it was a console table, a desk and a dining table all in one. The legs swivelled round both sides of the top, which was equally split into three and then folded up or down, depending on whether you were going to use it as a console (side) table, a desk where two of the three planks were utilised or a dining table where all three planks were in use. It was made out of thick chunky spotted gum timber that had mellowed beautifully in the decade or so since

I last saw it. So maybe, just maybe, they're still offering good service many years later for the original owner or its new custodian. I think there is a picture of it in the images section. Thankfully I'd learnt about tannins by this point.

There are countless stories about the workshop and one of them comes with a warning about its content. All will be revealed shortly but let's get back to James. As I said, I became good friends with James over the years, even working for him at one point after I shut down the studio when the GFC hit and Lyla was on the way. I needed to conserve cash and the prospect of a regular income compared with the choppy nature of being self-employed took priority. It was the same story over at James's: leaking workshop, tools crammed into impossible nooks and crannies, and more wood than you could shake a wooden stick at. So, it was business as usual as I took a lot of my tools over there with me and soon learnt how he operated. Operated being used in its loosest possible way for a descriptor of how it was run.

Another wet weather incident that will be indelibly etched into my mind I will describe now, but as mentioned previously, please bear in mind this should come with a warning of gory content. If this doesn't bother you, then read on. And if you skip ahead to the next chapter, you won't miss any huge revelation or insight I am about to reveal.

You'll know from previous paragraphs that before I took the step into the unknown – the world of furniture – I worked in the city, had a big circle of friends, socialised a lot and had a good standard of living. Following my dive into design I would say there were two factors driving my creations. Firstly, there were the client commissions that came easier and quicker than I had possibly imagined. This was obviously fantastic from a financial perspective but the other itch I wanted to scratch was making my own designs and building up my portfolio. As a result of the increased amount of time I was spending on client work, I was getting impatient at not being able to exercise my creative flair on my own work. So, after I had wrapped up a day's work and tidied up the workshop, I decided I would carry on for another hour or so although I was feeling tired. One adjustment I hadn't made to my life was my lifestyle. I was out drinking and smoking and carrying on as if I still worked in the city.

So there I am, at around 5pm, it's dark as it's winter and it's just me in my temple. I'm doing a special kind of cut on the saw and I keep getting it wrong due to my tiredness and lack of concentration, the lack of light in the workshop and the list goes on. Most tools I find are better suited to right-handed people. As a left-hooker I feel I am at an immediate disadvantage when operating anything. For example, the safety guard always seems to be in the wrong position, blocking your line of sight. The guide or fence is positioned on the wrong side to what feels instinctively natural. Any left-hander that is suddenly given a left-handed pair of scissors knows what I am talking about – and no, that is not a joke like asking to buy a left-handed hammer in the hardware store.

Most of my strength and dexterity are obviously being used on the tool back to front. So there I am, making a cut with the saw blade at full height for the equivalent of a tenon joint and the saw is bogging down due to the depth of cut required. I am watching the cut but need the strength of my left hand to pass the timber clear of the saw blade. Can you guess what's coming next? No prizes for guessing correctly. Only a centimetre or so to go so I give it a solid push and the workpiece tips over and I'm holding on tight so I can stop any kickback on the wood and the next thing I know there is a noise of an out-of-control piece of wood followed very quickly by the ring of a saw blade getting hit by something and then a feeling of zero resistance on what I'm working on. Any ideas why that lack of resistance occurred? I power down the machine and it takes a while for the blade to stop spinning and my mind is not immediately clear about what just happened. However, as I look down at the saw bed and go to move the piece of work I can see all is not as it should be. I attempt to pick up the piece of wood, but I struggle to get a grip of it and there is blood everywhere. This is all happening very quickly, you have to understand. Very quickly I realise I am now without a finger where there once was one and I have to start thinking. And think quickly. The saw has now stopped so there is silence in the workshop. I head over to the tap in the corner of the garage just behind the roller door and turn it on. Luckily some things I can do right-handed. I run water over the stump and find a cloth to tourniquet the wound, then run water over the rest of my hand to clean the blood off. It's only then I realise I've got another problem to deal with. As I turn my hand face up to wash my palm, I notice the thumb next to the now-not-there finger has an injury too: the tip of it falls back on itself and is only held on by the nail bed. It's a pretty full-on sight and I just go into survival mode. No time to think, just do. I wrapped the whole hand in a cloth, making sure to flick the thumb tip back into position before I wrapped it up tight.

Obviously I needed emergency assistance urgently. This time I wouldn't get away with going home with a bit of masking tape affixed to my hand. However, I couldn't for the life of me remember the three-digit code. You know, I've never in my entire life had to call them. In the UK, I knew it was 999 but never thought to memorise the Australian 000. So I rang the Vodafone directory enquiries 123 from my mobile to ask what the emergency number was. She was a bit confused by it all and patched me through. Not sure how I knew that number!

The rear lane that the garage backed onto was just a long line of other garages and there were no doors to people's homes. The garage was about halfway down the lane so to have gone all the way down to the bottom where the main road junction was to get help, I didn't consider. I wasn't really thinking straight. Anyway, the ambulance service was now on the line so I explained what happened but left out the whole left-handed people thing as it wasn't really necessary to the events that were unfolding, I surmised.

The lady on the line was lovely and asked a series of questions. I told her I was on my own so she said it was imperative I keep talking to her to keep me from going into a state of shock and that the ambulance would be there shortly. She did say quite categorically it would be very, very helpful to find the finger but its whereabouts was unclear. It was now dark and what limited light that existed in the garage was not really up to the task of finding missing fingers amongst piles of sawdust and tools. I looked all around the saw and surrounding the tool but it wasn't as though there was a tell-tale line of blood like a trail of breadcrumbs to follow, so it was anyone's guess where it had finally come down to land after getting spat out by the sawblade spinning at 2000rpm.

The equipment had a dust catcher but not a finger catcher, so that search proved fruitless. The emergency services were still on the line keeping me focused and although I knew it was important to find it, as the lady had also mentioned, the adrenaline would wear off at some point, which would expose my body to fatigue, pain and other unneeded emotions. Almost as if on cue, I slumped down onto the floor of the garage, which was soaking wet from yet more rain, and sat looking at piles of sodden sawdust with the undeniably crystal-clear thought of 'I really have gone and fucked it now' popping into my head. I think I told the emergency services lady as much. She was great and kept me focused and told me to keep looking for the finger, if at all possible. I said I'd try but was running out of ideas pretty quickly. She said that the ambulance was nearly there, and this was really the last chance. So, as I sat there in a puddle of water, very confused and not sure if I'd really run out of options, I looked up and at eye-level, on a small wooden ledge that I had built to house one of my tools, no more than two feet away, there was what looked like to my untrained medical eyes the remainder of my severed finger. My index or pointer finger, to be precise.

At that moment I was deliriously happy; in fact I would go as far as to say I have never been so happy to see my finger in all my life. It's not often you get that emotion from a finger and the feeling was like I was in some kind of altered state of reality.

My temporary altered state was quickly and abruptly interrupted as I reached out to pick up the welcome sight of an amputated digit. I hope you never ever have to go through this experience so you can take my word for this, but when you touch something that used to be part of you, it scrambles your brain. We all know what our own skin feels like to touch and like a fingerprint – no pun intended – it's unique to you. So, when something that was part of you until very recently is touched by something that is still part of you, your brain can't compute this and short-circuits itself. I was not prepared and had I been warned by the emergency operator that this would occur, I might have quickly fashioned up some chopsticks on the lathe to pick up my finger. I felt very woozy all of a sudden and nearly passed out right there on the drenched floor. Somehow, I kept my focus and tried to push away the thought that I had in fact passed out and finding the finger was part of some wicked dream I was having. The lady on the phone kept me talking and these thoughts passed. So, I wrapped it up in a few pieces of toilet roll and I honestly can't recall what happened next. I can remember very, very vaguely the ambulance racing though the city with sirens blaring and lights flashing on the way to the hospital. Or I may have imagined it, I'm not sure. What I do remember was Lauren marching into the waiting room at the hospital and saying to me, 'You've cut your f**kin finger off, haven't you?' I'm not sure if it was a genuine question that needed answering or a rhetorical one but either way, the morphine or pethidine they administered to me via the green whistle, was having quite the desired effect so nothing was making much sense anyway.

Later during my hospital stay, I would be told that I was found walking up the laneway towards the ambulance, clutching my wrapped-up finger and telling them I heard the sirens and saw the lights coming so set off to intercept them. I also had the presence of mind to turn off the power and lights, put the bins out, shut the roller door and snap the padlock shut, which was a hard enough ritual to achieve even with the full use of both hands – go figure. Amazing what the human body can do. I didn't remember a single thing and still don't –I only know it happened because they found the workshop that way.

Upon returning to the workshop many weeks later, whilst still healing and in rehab, I needed to slay the dragon before it consumed me so I grabbed the nettle and walked straight up to the machine, turned it on and made a simple cut. I needed to overcome my fear as soon as I could so it woodn't (deliberate spellie) overwhelm me and hold me back.

Surely the dog wood never bite its owner twice. One of the most difficult cuts I ever made was when I hung up my furniture-making boots many years later, before I moved into the business management side of the industry. I fired up the panel saw one last time and made a cut for the piece of furniture I was working on.

I walked away after making the cut and breathed a huge sigh of relief as it passed without incident.

What happened to the finger, I'm sure you're asking yourself? Well, for a joke the next Halloween I put it in a matchbox for the trick or treaters. No, no, no, that is a joke ... I put it in the Christmas pudding!!!!

On a serious note, they tried to reattach it as they have the medical skills through microsurgery to do so, but I'd done such a special job on it that even after reattachment there was no guarantee it would work or be successful. The side of it was pretty chewed up and besides, they needed flesh and other parts for the thumb, otherwise that would have to have come off too. All told, I made a full recovery and went back to furniture making. As a silver lining, whilst I was in hospital and having consults with the specialist he asked when I wanted to get back to work. I said, 'Err, like yesterday', as I had a ton of orders to get to. He asked if I smoked and I told him a doctor shouldn't really be smoking. He went on to explain that if I gave up smoking, I'd be back on deck in four weeks and if I carried on, it would be three months. I never smoked a cigarette again. Turns out the poison from cigarettes slows the body's ability to repair and fight potential infection. Get a bone infection and you're in deep poop.

Add another saying to the ever-growing list: 'Keep your fingers as long as you can for as long as you can.'

Even to this day my thumb is three millimetres shorter when placed side by side to the right, as the saw actually removes material, unlike say a knife cut.

There is another point worth dwelling on and that is the universe gives us plenty of warnings if we're going awry. I have described these warnings previously in the feather duster, brick and bus analogy. They are there to stop your momentum and get you to change course. I would say this was a brick moment and I changed course. I got serious with my work and realised the importance of adequate rest to balance work and play.

Another big learning that came to me over the period of having the business, which was totally unexpected and totally alien to me, was the psychological phenomenon called 'artist's rejection'. If you have not heard of this before, I will give you a one-paragraph explanation of it and how it affected me – and affect me it did!

Pursuing any creative endeavour is a fine tightrope walk between pleasure and pain. That is, the pleasure of making something amazing and then the pain when someone doesn't appreciate the effort that you have gone to to make the finished product. There were many occasions when I had poured my heart and soul into making, along with a lot of money, a bespoke item for a client, which I thought was amazing considering the brief I was given and the materials that I had to work with in some cases, only for them to be less than impressed with my output. Could have been a facial expression, verbally communicated or both.

Remember I left the corporate life of sales where I was a gun – with recognition and financial rewards showered down on me. Why would I leave that? Because I thought I could make it anywhere! Get all the recognition and achieve the financial success that comes with someone switching careers in their mid-30s to follow their life-long dream.

Oh, what a set up! So much so, if people didn't like what I was making or what I had made, or if I detected even the slightest hint of criticism, it was like a dagger through my heart. I couldn't believe it! It was a totally alien feeling to me and one that I was totally ill-prepared to deal with. Up until this time, I thought I was bullet-proof, remember? It would seem I would need even more armour, and more armour was what I put on. Coming back to earlier chapters, it is this very protection that stops people feeling and seeing the real you. It also stops you feeling the real you, which means that you can react to things and you don't even know why.

Looking back, this artist's rejection affected me considerably without me realising, including infiltrating my home life. Not just with Lauren, for example when I renovated the flat and she found fault in that but also in my relationship with Melinda when I had done things around the house. One ounce of any suggestion that things could be done a different way would hit home.

Even today I still suffer from it, for example, when writing this book I worried will people like it, have I written it well, etc? Such was and apparently still is my thirst for recognition! Why the need for all this recognition? Why do I have to keep proving my self-worth to the world? I know more and more that it could possibly be that we seek to complete ourselves outside of ourselves when in truth we are complete – inside and out!

I am much more aware of this now and am learning more and more that when you create something without expectation or emotional investment in the end result, you can be more detached and objective. One fellow creative, who suffered terribly also, described her reformed process as developing a project in step with the client – she now seeks feedback in real time as much as she can while developing what the client is after.

Regarding this book, it is for me first and foremost and also for my family and friends, but it is also for the wider public – humanity, if you go just that bit wider – as an offering of a good read but also there may be things that resonate, get readers to think about where they are at, the choices they are making and choices they have made. Would I like people to enjoy it? Absolutely, but since it was for me first and foremost, I'm okay if they don't. As I say at the end of the book: 'It has been an absolute pleasure to write this book as I did not set out to prove anything to anyone.' No perfection in this, of course!

So, there you have it, my early days of Maizon, moving out of Randwick and some of the learnings that have come from these experiences. In the next chapter you will see my drive and inventiveness get me onto prime time TV.

CHAPTER 16

Maizon Hits National TV

Oasis – Keep the Dream Alive (2015)

In this chapter I focus on the unique experience of getting my small garage start-up into every house in Australia – well, nearly!

HAVE YOU EVER heard the expressions 'you'll feel better in the morning' or 'sleep on it and see how you feel?'

I have heard that many people sleep with a notepad by their bed to capture their dreams or overnight thoughts. I would go to bed thinking of the issue I needed to solve from a design perspective and the solution would often pop into my head. Fortunately, I would remember a lot of what I needed to by the following morning. There was one instance, however, when I couldn't risk that not happening. I'm going to now tie the knot of two stories. You may remember me talking about one of the many nights I stayed up with Scarlett when she was very young.

During that time and being an entrepreneur with my business I started called Maizon, I learnt much about the mental side of becoming a businessman, not just the financial aspects. One of them was called artist's rejection, which I have described in the previous chapter. The second is a physiological condition whereby the creative part of your brain can go into a sort of hibernation mode. I was massively sleep-deprived, as many new parents are, and this was coupled with the stress of Scarlett's illness, and in situations like these, the brain prioritises vital functions, much like the flight or fight response you would have heard of before. Creativity for the purposes of survival is not considered a priority by the innate bodily functions, I was to find out. I've heard someone say that 'creativity is intelligence having fun'. Well, I can tell you there wasn't much fun happening in my life then. On the bed that night with Scarlett, when she was taking what seemed an eternity to get to sleep, I knew I had to find a way to keep the dream alive. I had to invent something that was based on my popular designs that I could get others to produce and allow me the time and space to get some much-needed recovery time. Essentially, I decided to make the move into mass production. Many of these challenges my body and mind were facing were total revelations to me, coming from the comfortable, cosy, closeted and cocooned world of corporate life. I'd already cut my finger off, as we know. I think the worst injury I had ever got at work up to that point was a paper cut on the photocopying feeder tray. As always, this new career path required me to navigate that all too familiar and by now well-trodden path of the steep learning curve. It was becoming natural terrain. Though the path was getting steeper and curvier.

So there I am, middle of the night, Scarlett delicately balanced in what seemed like the only position she was ever going to fall asleep in and one wrong move of just a single finger would send us back to the start of a screaming baby – a situation most if not all parents have been known to find themselves in. But I digress. I quickly put my brain into gear, cycled through a few ideas I had and then settled on one. Mentally reworked it a few times and once I knew Scarlett was asleep, I skillfully extricated myself from underneath her, taking the skill and delicacy of a bomb disposal expert trying to leave the scene of an unexploded bomb site, and tiptoed to go get the laptop. This was going straight to the submissions page on the ABC's *New Inventors* website. There were no iPhones with the kind of capabilities phones have these days, so getting to the lounge room before I fell asleep and lost it all forever was mission critical. I flipped open the laptop, wrote my idea and hit send. At that moment the Ezi-Shelf was born. I had approximately one minute to come up with the name before I hit send and fell into a deep sleep. I still kick myself that I could have done better with naming it on the submission to this day. Years later, after many reworkings of the original design, I wish I'd come up with the name Axis, to better reflect the important use of X that is used structurally in the design. By then it was too far in to change from its reworked Eco Shelf.

The New Inventors on the ABC was a bit of an institution. When I first met Mel, the story came up and she told me how much she loved the show and would often watch it. It ran for about eight series and I was on the last one – Mel unfortunately missed my one shot at the big time! It's now been discontinued, sadly. It was on at various times, but I remember 8pm on a Wednesday from memory.

In fact, a dear old friend from my teenage years back in Brighton named Julie happened to be watching on the very night I was on it and she had to do a double take as she couldn't believe what she was witnessing. Julie knew me from my much wilder exploits. She yelled at the TV to her family, 'That's Hillsy, that's Hillsy!' We reconnected and she has been instrumental in getting the book you are reading off the ground.

I can't tell you which day I submitted it, but I was in the studio one afternoon and my memory is a bit hazy on this, but either my phone rang or I opened the post and it was the ABC replying to my submission. They were interested in the idea and would like to send a couple of the production team over to take a better look. We spoke and I said, 'Yeah, sure, when do you want to come?' I certainly was not expecting the guy to say, 'How about tomorrow or the next day?' The ABC has its headquarters in Sydney, and they were near my studio and obviously keen to get a wriggle on with it. I had just expected a government broadcaster and a TV show to be a slow-moving pile of bureaucracy to overcome, but the guy firmed up a time to visit and the Ezi-Shelf wasn't just born, it was now attempting to crawl. I say crawl because the process of making anything and I mean anything, from a meal to a painting, to a sculpture, to a piece of music, should never ever be underestimated. Especially if it has never been done before. I've mentioned before I'm not trained in the traditional way, which does have its advantages but they are equally outweighed by its downsides.

I've since learnt that the process of inventing something, if there is even a process at all, is unlike anything you could possibly imagine. Say you were just going to build something for mass production and let's put aside for the moment it has never ever been attempted before, you may follow this process loosely:

First up, you need an idea/concept. Even coming up with the idea is not as straightforward as it sounds. I can't speak for others, as we all do things a bit differently. I use imagination a lot, others may find inspiration in another piece of furniture, others may even look outside the sphere of furniture making and draw on an idea from, say, nature or the shape of, say, a piece of architecture. It's not that important how you generate that creative spark, just that you generate it. The ethos of Maizon was and always has been that it had to at all costs be original. No plagiarising others' work, no matter how much easier it made the process. Let's use the example of a chef or a musician. I'm a complete dud, at both by the way. The chef might imagine the taste of the ingredients and know instinctively that they would work together. The musician might hear the sequence of notes and know that it would work.

Then, you need to turn it around in your mind. Whatever I am or was designing, I would imagine hundreds of different combinations in my mind. Much like one of those old-school handheld projectors, projected a moving image for the viewer. Visualisation is key here for me.

And then you need to get it down – commit it to the physical. Once I 'see' what I'm trying to create I will lock that image away, say by blinking, which will act like a camera shutter, and commit that to memory for future use. As I've said, I've no idea how others do it. Some may sketch, some may put a pile of wood on the bench and just experiment.

Incidentally, this is why I found it so hard to expand the business. I had plenty of hopefuls coming by the studio and asking if they could be involved and asking if I could teach them how to build some of these bonkers creations I was producing. But that's just it: you can't really teach it. It's about understanding materiality (fancy word for how materials go together from an aesthetic and practical perspective) and a healthy dose of pure imagination. The margin for error is astronomical. Imagine if you told someone to just 'see' it or 'taste' it or 'hear' it – they would think you had just arrived from Mars.

And then the process continues into prototype, testing, retesting and so on until full realisation of your concept. Well, here is how it panned out with the ABC.

The conversation continued and wrapped up with them agreeing to come by and take a look at the idea. Except that was just the problem – it was just that, an idea. I now had three days to turn the idea into something three-dimensional as described above.

The hard part. There was no such thing as rendering back then and even if I knew how to use AutoCAD, which I didn't, they wanted to see something physical. I decided I would use an old trick I'd seen used many times very successfully. The car industry does it a lot, as do architects, and that was to build a scale model. It could be done quickly and efficiently in my workshop. So, I set about creating this model, which turned out very well. Let's go back to the process of building something. Knowing what I know now, there are the following stages. 1 – Concept / 2 – Proof of Concept / 3 – Mock Up / 4 – Prototype or Rapid Prototype / 5 – Preproduction Prototype / 6 – Sample / 7 – Finished Product. The process between stages two and three usually cycles round and round for a while until the design is a bit more resolved. You could also exchange 1 – Concept for Idea but in reality, an idea still only exists mentally while a concept is at least drawn down or presented in some sort of 3D form but certainly not with working joints as the Ezi-Shelf required.

Essentially, I was starting from one and they were going to be here in two days' time. Anyway, as I said, the model went well. I've always been a big fan and collector of cigar boxes. The quality of the finish, the craftsmanship in the joints, the smell, the branding, it's all just exquisite. They make great storage cases too and I had plenty of them, so I chose an appropriate one, then I foam-lined it and might have even designed a little Ezi-Shelf logo and stuck it on the box. In fact, I still have that very cigar box with the model ensconced in its hand-cut foam padding. If it's possible, I will include it in the picture section of the book.

The guys from the TV show duly arrived and walked into the studio. They couldn't keep their eyes off a lot of the creations dotted around. They had doubtlessly been to hundreds of whacky places over the years all around the country as they chased down the next great invention that would solve some of the world's problems.

They spotted the floor lamp made from rolling pins, the table lamp made from old wooden tennis racquets, the lamp on the shelf made from an old SLR camera using the flash as a bulb, a tripod console table repurposing three antique cricket stumps as legs. The list went on. If you look closely, some of the pieces make their way into the final production trailer for the show. In the appendix section under Ezi-Shelf you will find the links to the videos etc. Their eyes lit up like a fruit machine on a winning reel nudge as they surveyed the scene. They sat at my desk (handmade by me, obviously) and we got chatting, and soon enough the topic turned to the Ezi-Shelf. I said that the pace of progress at their end had caught me a bit flatfooted and they explained that there was space in some upcoming episodes they wanted to fill. I pulled out my cigar box, flipped open the beautifully designed catch and took the pieces of the model out and built the approximate 1/10 scale model in front of them. Basically, the shelf worked by having a series of interlocking joints that could be dismantled or reassembled at a moment's notice. It all worked really well, and the guys were pretty impressed with what they saw. Along with the aroma of cigar and timber and varnish to fill the air, they wasted no time telling me how the filming could work and went through all the shots and angles and lighting. Then they asked where the actual shelf was so they could get an idea of scale. I delicately explained that I hadn't actually built it yet but that it would be okay as all the development work had been done. 'Yeah, right,' I said to myself. I asked what an appropriate size for filming would be. They gave some input into dimensions which were pretty much what I was envisaging the final piece to be. About two metres high by one metre wide. Then they dealt the hammer blow. 'OK, great,' they said as we were wrapping up. 'We'll be back in a week to see the shelf and start to do the filming.' 'A week,' I said in my coolest of cool voices. The Ezi-Shelf had just become the 'Im-possible Shelf'.

No sooner were they clear of the building, I was firing up the Stag and tearing across the city to the timber yard, my mind doing all manner of calculations and considering all the permutations for what now needed to be done. This was it, the moment I'd been waiting for. Finally, the recognition I so desperately craved. I still had a bunch of client orders to finish and deliver. Oh yes, I also had a baby under 12 months old to care for. I still needed to desperately catch up on some much-needed sleep. What is it they say about motion creating emotion? Well, in for a penny, in for a pound. God, I was excited. One of the reasons I found Sydney so conducive to starting the business was the proximity of the essential ingredients to feed the life force of its existence, namely, raw materials (the timber yard), a place to produce my magic (the workshop/studio) and my clients (residential and small business owners). All these could be found within a two-kilometre radius of my studio in Darlinghurst. Five minutes after I'd waved goodbye to the TV reps, I was parked up at the timber yard going through the racks and, sifting through metre upon metre of hardwood, telling anyone who would listen, 'I'm going to be on prime-time national TV' and to be frank, even if they weren't listening, I still told them anyway!

I finished off the design in my head as I was ferreting around in the wood racks, then paid and went and loaded up the car. This was my on the job development work! I took my haul of timber straight back to my studio like a predator with a fresh kill making for a safe exit. I wasted no time getting down to work and after a few simple miscalculations, I was on my way to having something loosely resembling what I would present on the show sitting on my workbench. You could say that stages 1 through to 4 (Idea to Rapid Prototype) were done. It was about two hours since the TV guys had left. The clock was ticking ...

So far, so good. Then I made a huge misstep by canvassing another opinion. Buoyed by the series of events, I went to see a guy called Ross Longmuir who owned Planet Furniture. It was very nearby and I admired his work enormously, so whilst I was running around, I took my model and went to see him. I knew he'd been on the show before with his 'intersection' shelving unit. I got straight down to business and immediately started showing him and telling him what I was up to. He was a great sounding board. In no time, however, he very cleverly picked up my two uprights, turned them 180 degrees and re-slotted them, thereby creating another configuration of a low, wide shelf and not just the tall, thin one I had envisaged. It left me with a big dilemma. Stick with the original concept or go with the now expanded idea. Well, being the sort of guy who doesn't complain about the noise if opportunity knocks, I went straight back to the timber yard to buy more wood. It was getting time-consuming and expensive. This is why on the video you see two versions of the shelf, even though it was never intended to happen like that. Great – I had just created twice the work for myself. The TV crew would be delighted though.

The week deadline was fast arriving but I did now at least have a working prototype – in fact I had two – so I was feeling confident about the filming. Then I had the most severe attack of gastro that saw me bedridden for a day at least. Time I could ill afford to lose but as I would come to understand, the body shows signs of stress in all sorts of ways and this was one of them, telling me to stop and rest when my mind was not willing!

The day of filming in my studio arrived. I was back in rude health and raring to go. The crew of two turned up bang on time and unloaded all the kit. There was a lot of it. They even had one of those fancy train tracks for taking the camera up and down for super-steady motion shots. They had already made a script for me to follow, which I eagerly studied and started rehearsing. This was my big moment, remember. Couldn't even consider the notion of mugging my lines. All I needed was a 'filming in progress' sandwich board out the front to announce to the world what was going on. Lauren came by with Scarlett, who they thought was imperative in the shots. You can see her wobbling around in her buggy, looking up at me when I speak. Don't they say never work with children? That's about all I know about filming. These guys were great, so that rule clearly didn't apply to them. The half day it took to film for just a minute for the broadcast episode makes you realise why filming and photography are so expensive. I've got no idea of the cost, but that segment would have to be $10K of free production. It was a lot of fun and after a few hours they were done; it's a wrap, as they say. Had to drop that line in, didn't I?

So, it was on to the ABC Head Office and filming in front of a live audience of about 250 people, I seem to recall. Countdown since submitting and sending the application on my design would be now approximately two weeks. A ridiculously short space of time to have a product conceptualised and built, ready to film in front of a live audience. I had no idea what to expect. Sure, I'd seen the show numerous times so knew the format well but nothing really ever prepares you for the moment you walk out onto the stage beneath the bright lights and start talking. You can't imagine the feeling. Earlier in the day I'd loaded up the Stag as usual but this time headed the other way to normal and drove the short distance to the ABC into an entrance marked 'Stage Deliveries'. It all felt pretty special. I unloaded the shelf in its flatpack form and reparked the car. It was probably about 2pm at this stage and behind the scenes I met the other two inventors who were going to be filmed with me. One was a very young girl in her late teens who had designed a special tool to get all the mud out of the difficult-to-reach parts of a motocross bike. This is a problem that needs addressing, especially where water can't be used to hose the bike down. The other was a guy of a similar age to me who had come up with a special heart-rate monitor thing. Not sure exactly what it did or how it did it. All in all, a very diverse collection of inventions.

The studio at the ABC wasn't the intimidating place I imagined it to be and I was so psyched about getting in front of the cameras and the show's audience that any trace of nerves or anxiety were, if they even existed, soon replaced by pure excitement.

I met the host who had been the front man for the show for as long as I could remember, a lovely guy called James O'Loughlin. I didn't meet the judging panel of three industry experts until filming commenced. We did a few dress rehearsals earlier in the day to get the camera and light angles correct but my dialogue wasn't rehearsed and I had to ad-lib it all.

It was during one of these dry runs that the tools had to suddenly come out again. I had the height of the spacing between the shelves worked out for one of those demo plastic TVs you find in furniture stores (to show how a piece of furniture would look with a TV on it or in it) but the ABC was licensed to only use a certain brand and the one they had didn't fit in the space.

So, I was back on the tools once more, round the back of the stage area with some basic equipment to make the shelf work as intended. Then suddenly it was lights, camera, action. They really do say, 'Cameras rolling and action.' James was very good at guiding the filmed sequence and as far as I can remember, no retakes were required. I knew the shelf inside out and had no problem setting it up and adjusting it on demand, as well as answering all the questions despite the very basic run-through beforehand.

Then it was over to the expert panel for their questions and the three of them were a bit of a mixed bag. One of the guys was super encouraging and really easy to engage with, but of course the format of the show was such that someone had to play the devil's advocate. One of the female judges took up that role and got straight into the negatives, questioning the choice of product name and criticising the design. I didn't feel it was appropriate on national TV to explain to her that I came up with it when I was sleep-deprived and that the producers of the show only gave me two weeks to finalise everything before my appearance and when I did finally appear, they threw me a curveball and got me to re-make it out the back in 30 minutes flat. I thought it but didn't say it. Nonetheless, it all went smoothly and I was extremely buoyed by the comment by the other female judge: 'Well, Philip, I think you should be expecting a call from a certain large Swedish furniture company.'

What happened next? Despite my best efforts over many years and a huge amount of perseverance, I could not get a response from this large Swedish furniture company. I poured hundreds more hours into the project, bored two successive partners with my unrelenting zeal to get it off the ground, but manufacturing in Australia proved impossible and finding quality producers in China even more so. In this time, the GFC hit, relationship issues that were simmering since the birth of Scarlett were compounded by the health issues of my second daughter Lyla (which you have read about) and resulted in the end of our de facto relationship (not because of the shelf, I might add here!). I built my second corporate career, this time in the high-end furniture industry, found love again and finally Covid put the nail in the shelf's coffin when China shut its doors in 2020. We do have a beautiful finished product of the now called Eco-Shelf sitting pride of place in our lounge room. A leftover of one of the best prototypes that was made in China when looking for a manufacturer. We love it!

However, at this point in the book it is important to say that there were some commercial successes within business.

From earlier chapters you will know that I had many, many different pastimes and hobbies. One of them was skateboarding, which was immensely popular in the 70s and 80s. But due to my humble background, it was not always possible to buy the latest skateboard. Being practical though, I turned my hand to making them. One feature of a skateboard that everyone will recognise is called the kicktail, which is the tail end of the board. This seemingly innocuous part of the board is actually from an engineering point of view a very difficult design element to achieve. My first prototype was just cut from a flat piece of plywood. I was so pleased with it that upon presenting it to my friends for its inaugural outing, I performed my go-to favourite trick, which was jumping off a wall at about shoulder height, having the board under my feet and landing on the pavement. I am sure there is a name for that trick these days but back then it was just the 'off the wall' trick. I landed the trick but much to my dismay, the kicktail snapped off. My mates and I all stood around howling with laughter as I realised another method was required. Upon reaching home, Dad commented that the plywood I used was too thin but actually what I found was that it needed to be thinner but from layers of it in a laminating process. Basically, I ended up gluing a lot of thin pieces of plywood, putting them into a clamp and pressing them into a curved shape. This action of layering the plywood not only made the structure stronger but allowed me to create the all-important curve of the kicktail. I tentatively tried the 'off the wall' trick again – this time to my amazement, it held solid. I think the phrase in design is 'fail fast, learn quick'. Through my first endeavour I inadvertently came across the solution – bending the tail and making the skateboard stronger simultaneously. Oh, I would love to have gone into skateboard-making at the time but I was only 13. You also have to remember that the majority of kids in that era were riding around on plastic lollipop stick boards as they were called, so the industry was ripe for developing wide wooden boards. It was just around the corner.

Nevertheless, I was able to put this experience to good purpose ... back to Maizon.

One day a guy from a very nice furniture shop from around the corner to my studio came in and told me he had a problem with one of his suppliers and could I replace him. I said, 'Sure, no problems.' 'Great, stop by the shop and I'll tell you what needs doing,' he replied. On my next outing I stopped by and he showed me a beautiful bent plywood coffee table. The moment I looked at it, I immediately thought of two skateboards joined end to end. I agreed to make one for him to look at. As with all these things, the first one took a lot longer to make than I first envisaged. My self-taught seven-step process would prove invaluable. The finished product was worth it though and what followed was a relationship spanning many months making these bespoke curved-end coffee tables for my friend around the corner. It also became a signature piece for my studio. Unfortunately, he went out of business not long after with the GFC. I was able to keep going longer due to the low overheads that I had. But ultimately, I had to get out too, as I was needed more at home with the children growing up fast and I needed to conserve my cash reserves. This was when I started working with James who you met in the previous chapter.

So, from my humble tinkerings as a child and teenager in my grandad's shed and then my dad's workshop, I was able to turn this into a workable business. I was able to let my creativity shine and I loved it. Would I have loved to have kept it going longer? Yes, of course, but life didn't allow for that at the time. I've always strongly believed in the saying, 'If you love what you do, you will never have to work a single day in your life.' Had I had more time to build my business before circumstances were thrust upon me, I believe I could have made my adult tinkering financially viable long-term.

My restless inventiveness has never left me, as Mel would attest to. I always had some project on the go – big or small. I made a daybed on the stairwell landing of our townhouse, making use of existing shelves that activated the space into a liveable area we all used. At the start of the first Covid lockdown in 2020, Mel jumped to the sound of the hammer going through one of the walls that I found superfluous to the flow of the kitchen, which then started a remodelling of this space. Even to this day Melinda's dad still marvels at my creative abilities in using previously unused space. I also made my girls' beds at our place and custom-built Lyla's bed in her Randwick home.

PART FIVE

WHAT HAVE I LEARNT?

In these last two chapters, I bring you to my more recent years and what I have learnt through the process of writing this book.

CHAPTER 17

❦

Right Before My Eyes

Fatboy Slim – Right Here, Right Now (1999)

This chapter is about waking up to find that all those so-called loves of my life like cars, furniture-making and music were just a tad superficial and my real love was right there before me. Melinda, my beautiful wife. Well, she has to be beautiful really, as the name 'Melinda' apparently means 'my beautiful lady' in Spanish.

I THINK IT'S FAIR to say that most of us have a type when it comes to the opposite sex, but Mel was completely different to my usual type in so many ways. Super natural, super practical and super down-to-earth.

I distinctly remember a conversation I had with her very early on, maybe in the first or second week of seeing each other and it turned to our beliefs about the bigger-picture stuff. A thought she shared about religion and Christianity was one of the most believable I'd ever heard in my life. As far as she knew there was a guy called Jesus, and he was a pretty amazing guy who had lived and spoken a tangible truth. Whether he did all the amazing miracle-style things that the Bible attests to and if he indeed rose from the dead, who knows, but he was persecuted and he was betrayed. I found this version of events far more believable and something I could settle with, rather than the stories institutionalised religion teaches.

Melinda also shared with me around this very early time that a lot of her old habits, such as social drinking, were something that she was on a path to eradicating. She asked if this was going to be a problem for me. I certainly was no raging alcoholic then but I still nudged it a bit on the weekends. As you know, I had done my fair share of drinking, smoking and drug-taking in my life. I had given up smoking and drug-taking long ago and I had recently even given up my very strong addiction to sugar – well, at least had given it a serious shaking. I had also started to regularly go to the gym as I was no longer 'on the tools' as it is oft described in the furniture industry and was working a more sedentary office role at Space Furniture, so the exercise was good. I was approaching the age of 45, heading towards my 50s and certainly had a few bad habits of my own to drop, so hitching my wagon to hers was not a hard decision. There were some bumpy roads and some gentle and then not-so-gentle reminders of where she was heading and so, if I was heading there with her, I needed to shape up. In our first few years together, I realised I needed to get my house in order, which I was more than happy to do. So much so that when I was diagnosed with terminal brain cancer mid-2021 at the age of 49, after five years of being together, I was the fittest, cleanest, healthiest and most balanced I had been in my life.

Another area of Melinda's personality that I found engaging early on was the fact that not only was she fit and active and she liked sport, she knew about sport. This was not like other girlfriends who, although they looked after their bodies, were not actually sporty per se. Melinda and I would go to sporting events together, and follow a lot as well, and we thoroughly enjoyed this aspect of our relationship until it wasn't as important anymore.

Being a farmer's daughter, Mel was extremely practical. This I found very refreshing. She even owned a toolbox! Of course she did! When asking if she had one when I had to fix something and not expecting a positive response, out came this cute little Ikea tool set that became my favourite go-to from then on. She washed her own car and even bought and sold her cars herself, something that my exes had no idea about. Not that this is an indictment on them, just that it was amazing to sit back and see Melinda do so much of her life for herself rather than relying on a man in her life. This independence, I found very attractive.

I was one of those traditional kinda guys in my early years when it came to relationships. I thought it was my role to be the provider, no questions asked. Even though I was very much a 'work hard, play hard' guy, I was always super respectful of women. In relationships I put myself forward as my partner's go-to person, to be the dependable and consistent one in their life. The problem with that way of thinking, however, was that when that person didn't appreciate what I was doing for them, it would be incredibly hurtful for me. Instead of being able to express this and chat openly about what I was feeling, reactions would unfortunately often take over.

As Melinda was already independent and complete without me, our relationship started on a very different footing to other relationships. One without needing the other to fill a void. Sure, we had our ups and downs and we didn't do it alone. We got help when we needed to unravel the knots we found ourselves in from time to time, especially in the early days, and we were also dealing with a split family. We both had previous lives, of course, mine including two children! And Melinda came from years of not finding a suitable partner to settle down and have a family with. She brought her baggage and that was okay: I brought mine too!

We gradually learnt that our hurts from years and years gone by, including from our childhood and adolescence, drive our reactions which in the end are not us. Not only did we do the practical things like giving up drinking, as well as caffeine and a lot of processed foods, we gave up the emotional rollercoaster rides by not identifying ourselves with our hurts. We both evolved and matured together, side by side. Again, no perfection of course and still much to let go of but on that note, due to being in such good health mentally, emotionally and physically with amazing supports around us, it has allowed me/us to deal with this illness in ways that I would never have thought possible.

Without the physical changes I had made to my life, I truly believe that I wouldn't be still sitting here writing this book now, 19 months on from the original diagnosis. This cancer has a general prognosis of under one year. My oncologist was a bit more generous and gave me 18 months, given the particular cellular makeup of my tumour – needless to say, I'm on borrowed time now.

In April 2016, Melinda and I met the 21st-century way – via a dating app! Melinda was my Tinderella and I was her Tinderfella. Later, Melinda mentioned that on the night she met me she had come with absolutely no expectations but with an open heart and mind; having dated a few people online, she knew what not to do and that is to project! Apparently, this was very important for her as she also later shared that she spotted a ring on my wedding finger very early on in the evening and questioned in her head, 'How and why on earth does a married man so blatantly go on a date while he is married?!' She also shared later that her first impressions were of this gorgeous man, snappy dresser with plenty of charisma but looked like a bit of a party boy. Let's just say, she had some questions poised but she didn't have to pose any as I came straight out with my story, that I had recently separated from a long-term relationship from which I had two daughters (at the time three and six years old) and that yes, I loved a party in my early years but who has the time for that stuff now, etc. She recalls that I didn't stop talking for about the first half hour and that my abridged life story allayed any fears she had. The rest of the night, as they say, is history!

The ring, I might add, was one I fashioned out of a nut and it just happened to sit on my wedding finger as my ex and I did not get married. Melinda and I used a simple wedding band for our marriage so there is now a bona fide wedding ring on my wedding finger.

My first impression of Melinda was a breath of fresh air. Her pictures online were not curated. One particular one was of a simply beautiful woman sitting on the grass at a picnic. I appreciated the honesty and transparency apparent in Melinda; mind you, she was also rocking a cute short skirt in this particular pic! She postponed our first meeting because of work commitments and made me wait, as after that she was off on a family holiday to Tasmania. In this time we got to message each other a bit prior to actually meeting. When we finally met, it was at a bar/restaurant local to Melinda in Balmain, and I booked a table inside as she had let me know she had not dressed for the cooler autumn eve that it was. She wore a slinky white camisole atop a slimline pencil skirt. With her gorgeous blue eyes and rich, bountiful locks of hair, she had me at hello!

On a deeper note, throughout our relationship Melinda set a standard, a standard that I didn't think I was up to initially, but she continually asked of me to be a better man. She did not allow me to be anything less than I am capable of being and I am so glad I was open to this. In the past, the old me would have said, 'If you don't like it, lump it.'

I feel that one of the positives I have brought to Melinda's life is the reaffirming in her of her innate sexiness that can be swamped sometimes by all that practicality. Over the years I have bought her clothes, either online or from shops where something catches my eye as I pass by. Clothes she absolutely loved but would not have bought herself. Initially she was in awe that I could pick items of clothing that not only fitted perfectly but looked great! Over time she started to veer towards these styles herself and it is absolutely gorgeous to see her reclaiming this part of her being. Too many women have too much self-doubt and it is crushing to see, so I am glad Melinda has been open to me and what I brought to our relationship.

We have done a lot in our short time together, including many trips away to beautiful places in Australia, Byron and Hobart being faves, but interestingly it has been these recent months that we have spent together, both in hospital and at home, that have deepened our relationship. That first fateful weekend in hospital when I was diagnosed, the weekend of Scarlett's 12th birthday, we talked, we cried, we held each other and we were blanketed by the support of our family and friends – we were and continue to be so held. This moment in time changed our lives forever and the deepening of us as individuals and as a couple commenced in earnest. Life has become about the small things – the otherwise mundane things like driving to pick up the girls from school, taking them to sport, having a simple meal out or our regular Saturday morning cuppa up the road. Life is indeed not about sweating the small stuff but about every single moment, however small, and bringing quality to those moments. Again, with no perfection.

I had a fear though that I always held in my relationship with Melinda, prior to my diagnosis obviously, that if shit was ever to get really real one day, like something really big/monumental happened, she wouldn't have the smarts or composure to cope with the situation. Mel in our early years wasn't always so good about not sweating the small stuff as in the line above. She had her panic pants firmly planted in her baggage that she brought along and kept within easy reach. She knew this and was working on it but I can now say holus-bolus that I stand fully corrected on my assumptions regarding her ability to cope or not, as she has been an absolute rock of stability and unwavering support that I can honestly say I could not have managed without. Many hospital nights I lay awake thinking of this exact scenario – that I could not possibly have managed without her.

It is this story that brought us to getting engaged and committing to marriage.

I will now take you back to August 2021. I had just started a six-week course of daily chemotherapy and five days a week of whole brain radiation sessions. It was two full weeks post-surgery to remove the main walnut-sized tumour from my right temporal lobe. I had recovered incredibly well from the surgery, and the steroids that they put you on straight away post-op fuelled my initial enthusiasm for writing this book but as the steroids were withdrawn and treatment started in earnest, I very soon found myself back in hospital. I didn't even last the first week.

During that first week, I was still working full-time but with provisions and modifications and I would spend the last hour of the day sitting at my desk in the girls' room, writing the start of this book. Mel would be in the kitchen, which was adjacent to the girls' room, preparing dinner. The first day of treatment I was floored with a mother of all headaches that thankfully responded to a good few hours of sleep in the afternoon. On the second day of treatment, I came out of my so-called office to read Mel my latest contribution. I placed the computer on the bench and went to get some water out of the fridge when something took my left arm and lifted it into the air and then proceeded to take my whole body to the side, so much so it was like I was being dragged into our lounge room. Mel immediately stopped what she was doing to come and hold me as we were both guided by this apparently mysterious force to the lounge and sat down. We looked at each other and said, 'What was that?!!!' My hand and face began tingling; it was scary stuff. But as soon as it had come, it had gone again. I had been complaining of a lot of tension in my neck and shoulders in recent days and I thought it was just still getting over the surgery and working at the computer more. What we were not aware of was that these were signs and symptoms of partial seizures, most probably caused by the radiation treatment and the surgery. What followed were many days of sporadic spasms and seizures, which eventually took away my ability to walk as the seizures gradually worsened despite my being hastily put on anti-seizure medication. The medications didn't seem to touch the sides and unfortunately, a major side effect is that you can become incredibly emotional. So not only was I losing my independence very swiftly, which would make any grown man cry, the medications amplified this. By Sunday it was no longer feasible for me to stay at home. Robert, Mel's dad, and Mel safely got me to hospital for the second time and again being Covid, I was alone presenting at RPAH emergency. Fortunately, the Lifehouse, where I had my original surgery, allowed one loved one to come in so it was not long before I was transferred back to there and Melinda was by my side again.

This was the start of an eight-week hospital stay for me to complete the rest of my treatment and recover to a state where I was safe to go home. It was huge!

Day after day, night after night, the seizures were relentless, despite increasing levels of medication that should have kicked in by now. The issue with bringing seizures under control is that you have to titrate the medications up gradually, so this delay between beginning a new regime of medication and seeing the effect was not only time-consuming but also incredibly scary as the cancer treatment marched along at its exact pace. There was no changing the treatment schedule despite the alarming effect it had on body and brain. It looked cruel on the outside to Melinda and it was downright terrifying on the inside. As Mel did her best to advocate for me as the days wore on, there was somewhat of a surrender to the process. I gradually lost my ability to walk completely, to sit up, shower and even go to the toilet myself. I was totally dependent on all around me and especially Melinda, who was there for over six hours each day during the working week and longer on weekends. She lovingly left me to sleep around 9pm each evening and despite being on the biggest and best medications to help me sleep with my seizures, the nights were long and hard.

One very memorable night in hospital became known as The Night of 1000 Seizures between me and the team of specialists and doctors who were looking after me during my stay. On this particular night I went to sleep as per usual with a dose of Clonazepam, a heavy sedative to help with the seizures but, as with anything in the 'Pam' family of drugs, your body gets used to them and they become less effective with time. You effectively build a tolerance to them so you need greater and greater doses. Instead of being able to sleep through the night on one dose of the drug, I would often wake again in the middle of the night. This night, I pressed the buzzer to ask for another dose, only to be told by the nurse I had hit the limit of the scheduled amount. I was left in the frightening situation where I was now wide awake, the seizures were coming thick and fast and my thoughts were running riot. At one point in the night, around 3 to 4 in the morning, with the fear well and truly upon me, I lay there thinking this could well be the night that my life was going to end. I steadied myself and made a mental note that if I was to make it through the night alive, I would propose to Melinda. The fear was dripping through the ceiling but, somehow, I found a few hours of sleep despite the seizures apparently continuing. Let's just say I have never been so pleased to hear morning birdsong and see the sun rise over the horizon through my hospital window, after what was one of the worst nights of my life. I had many a bad night in hospital but this was by far the worst. Morning also heralded a new schedule of drugs that might help bring these seizures under control for at least a few hours' reprieve!

While in hospital, Melinda and I were able to talk about a lot of things, particularly how our life together would be going forward. During this time our relationship grew stronger and stronger. There were good moments, when it seemed I had turned the corner, like the first time I sat out of the bed again, the first time I was able to shower myself again, the first time I dressed myself and the first time I stood again. These were all amazing moments that we shared together. I even celebrated my 50th birthday in hospital and the girls were allowed to visit. I was able to sit in the wheelchair to go to radiation for the first time that day and amazingly I was able to sit upright in a chair the whole time the girls were there that night. We had Thai takeaway in a box and a beautiful cake. Not my planned 50th, where we were going to go skiing in Victoria for the week, but I was just so glad to be alive and be with my girls.

We spoke with both the palliative care doctor and the social worker who gave us an insight into what might be ahead and it was apparent we needed to sell our three-storey townhouse. This meant leaving behind my three-car garage and workshop but gaining a beautiful newish apartment with seamless inside–outside living that I would find essential as my mobility had declined so much. Those conversations in hospital were incredibly supportive for us and meant that I have had an amazing place in which to recover, undergo treatment and face the next phase.

By the time we got to selling our place, I was gradually able to start moving around without the wheelchair. During the first open house, we put the commode I was using and the wheelchair down in the garage. We never brought it back up again as I quickly learnt how to get around more and more without it and became stronger. A common stroke recovery treatment is to restrain the 'good arm' so the person is forced to use the arm that the brain is not firing so well to. You have to relearn how to use the limb and it has been shown to be quite effective. Not having the wheelchair available anymore can be likened to this strategy and meant that I had to use what I had – and it worked!

I was still not able to walk any major distance though and mostly needed support. Melinda came home one morning from the shops and triumphantly reported that she had found a lovely ring up the road at the jewellers and that we should get it and put it on the wedding finger. I was totally aghast! I was just about to propose myself but my moment was taken! We still laugh at the timing of those events even today. Mel earned the title from me as the 'unstoppable force' and with my disabilities, I named myself the 'immovable object'. Melinda was in the hot seat to win that battle of physics!

Incredibly, we moved into our new place close to three months after my discharge from hospital. Melinda really was the unstoppable force! Having achieved so much, we bought the ring in celebration – Mel did take me up there prior to the move to show me the ring and I loved her choice – a gorgeous green tourmaline stone in a simple gold band. I ended up proposing twice, once in front of her mum and step-dad, Geoff, and again the next night in front of her dad and step-mum, Les. The perfect end to a most harrowing time.

Then Melinda was off again and wasted no time organising a super simple wedding of 20 at a local rotunda in Elkington Park in Balmain, the home of the iconic Dawn Fraser Pool, and then down to a beautiful waterfront restaurant overlooking the Harbour Bridge at Balmain East. She had amazing help from friends, family, the local community, even the council was on our side! Even so, I still couldn't understand the rush to have the wedding. Couldn't we just settle into our new place for a while? But I am so glad she did what she did when she did as I was able to walk easily down the path with her, flanked by her father and step-father. It was a beautiful, very special occasion that no more than a few months after I would not have been able to do. We had a very, very fun and joy-filled day. It was a moment in time that was exactly at the right moment in time. My parents came out from England for the event at the ripe old age of 80 – amazing! We all went on a 'family moon' to Port Macquarie the following week, which will now always be a very special place for us.

We have been back since but for me, my travelling has now finished. Having travelled the world with what seems like only snippets described in this book, I will have finished my last years with little trips up and down the east coast of Australia but as mentioned, in Australia, every day is a holiday. I felt that from the moment I arrived here and I still feel that strongly. The apartment we ended up buying is on Sydney Harbour. Our building faces west and the water but our apartment faces north and looks out onto other buildings in the complex. There are big glass sliding doors that make up the walls on the north and east sides so we are effectively living in a fish bowl! For me, it is great as I spend a lot of my time looking out on the various goings on and the beautiful expansive sky. There are days now where I am unable to get out of the house, soon to be many more, but I love it. If I had to pick where I would be spending my last months and days, I couldn't have done a better job. We think it was heaven sent!

We are coming up to our one-year wedding anniversary and our time together has been exquisite, incredibly special. It is absolutely beautiful to be sharing our life together. To the love of my life as Philip Hills – I love you, Melinda.

CHAPTER 18

---∾---

The Burden of Proof

London Grammar – Wasting My Young Years (2013)

*This chapter is where I tie it all together and see what I have
learnt – about life and about death.*

I WAS BORN Philip Richard Hills on the 2nd of September 1971
(oh, how many times have I had to write, say or confirm this
date over the last year and a half being in the medical system!?).
I write it here as I now know that I was born complete and will die
complete, in all probabilities before my 52nd birthday. Did I live in
the knowing that I was complete? The answer to this is a definite
no up until this last year or so. Would it have made a big impact
on my life if I did? Yes, absolutely. Why? Because I have come to
learn or realise it is often this feeling of lack of completion that
drives us forward and makes us think we have to prove ourselves.
I'm not saying here that you lie back and think life is done for you
but I am saying that without drive or having something to prove
that I could have definitely been a whole lot kinder to myself
as well as those around me. Without these two willing suspects
behind me throughout my life, I could have been in the flow of life,
responsive to what came up for me and followed where my heart

and soul took me, rather than being in the rush of having to make it for myself. I do believe looking back at my life there were periods where I let this inner self/sense guide me, particularly in the last year. Whenever I have gone into drive over the last year, trying to work it all out, I have become exhausted as my brain has become like an old iPhone with its battery life just about all used up, no matter how many times you charge it. I have had to do life a different way and this takes us back to the start of the book when I mentioned that I didn't want to battle cancer. I wanted to surrender to what was needed and take out the lessons to be learnt from this year and a half. I have done this – without perfection, as you will read over this coming chapter.

But before I get too far in, where did this chapter's title come from? As those of you in the legal profession will know, the 'burden of proof' is where the prosecutor in a case must prove beyond reasonable doubt that the accused is guilty, in other words innocent until proven guilty. For me in this book, it is as if I have lived my life as a prosecutor bringing their case against myself on a daily basis where I developed a need to prove myself, to myself, to my family and loved ones, to my work colleagues, to my friends, to my so-called enemies and to the world. But I am here, alive to tell everyone – to exclaim it from the highest vantage ...Yes, I am worth it!!!

But all along I was. There was no need to gather evidence, no need for the burden of proof.

Hence the title of the book: *The Man Who Tried to Prove Too Much.*

Looking back, I can now see how too much of my life in the past was trying to prove who I was in the world. Prove to myself, or to others, that I could make it in the world.

So why was this? Why did I feel I needed to prove my worth to the world? Why does anyone?

Let's go back to the original question posed at the start of the book.

To save you the trouble of finding it, I'll rewrite it here.

What is drive, where does it come from and why do some of us have more of it than others?

There is the physical act of driving which, as you would have read, formed a huge part of my identity as a classic car freak, so when this was taken away from me, you can understand I was in a world of hurt. To say I have become more sensitive in the last year is an understatement. But then again, that is who we truly are as well, super sensitive. Why is it that a man needs to build an outer armour of toughness, hardness, that the process of a young boy growing up is one where you learn to toughen up, to not show your emotions, to succeed in life. When again, at our core is absolute sensitivity, and that is actually a power house in itself. I have returned to that sensitivity – for example, I can no longer be in front of people who do not talk with a certain level of honesty about themselves and to be honest, I can no longer be in front of people who only talk about their material gains. Not because I can no longer build mine, but because there is no depth there.

Back to the physical act of driving. As soon as I had brain surgery mid-2021, my licence was taken away due to the risk of seizures. As mentioned in the last chapter, I didn't have to wait long before that eventuated. I was given my licence back about one year later after the seizures had well and truly been brought under control by a daily cocktail of medications. However, no sooner was my licence back in my hands, I lost the use of my right leg and with it any dream of getting back to driving. We don't quite know the reason for losing the use of my leg, but not only could I not drive anymore but I lost the ability to walk any meaningful distance as well. This was again consolidated when in December last year I seemed to have another step down regression and I have required the use of a wheelchair when I am home by myself and when I go out to any appointment or social occasion. Talk about a humbling process that I had to, in my own time, come to terms with. I did drive around our basement car park – Mel and I would swap drivers at the entrance to the common garage where we now live and I would drive down and park my car. No more after June last year as I could no longer control my right foot. This classic car tragic is not able to drive anymore. So, in this definition of drive – I'm out.

To keep with the car analogy one more moment, I mentioned in one of the previous chapters that looking back throughout my life I can see I was using the wrong kind of fuel. Just like any engine, the human body needs fuel to drive it. Put the wrong fuel in a car and it coughs and splatters or it just doesn't go. For the human body, it can keep going and going but the quality in which you do things suffers. I used the energy of drive to fuel me and while it didn't make me cough and splutter at the time, it did make me stop when my body said enough – and the proverbial bus hit me! A lot of people wonder, 'Why me?' when they are diagnosed with a terminal illness but others find meaning in it. For me it was to stop a momentum I was in for possibly lifetimes. I had dodged the feather dusters, taken on the bricks and now it was time for the bus to get me to sit up and listen.

I think for a lot of us, drive is another word used for acting with motivation to garner success in life – whatever that means to a person. But is drive a genuine representation of a part of one's character or is it a series of layers that a person develops over time to protect themselves? Which then goes somewhere to answering the next part of the question – why do some of us have more of it than others?

If the drive comes from protecting yourself, then what follows is that some people may have more hurts and fears than others that they feel they need protection from. A typical way of describing this may be by saying that a person is insecure, but I think it goes deeper than that.

As you have read, my hurts and fears were key drivers for most of my life. I wanted to cover up for the lack of recognition I felt in my early years; I wanted to secure my life financially so I did not have to depend on anyone as I didn't think anyone could be depended upon; I wanted a loving relationship to gain the love and acceptance I felt I deserved but most importantly I wanted to fill the gap between who I was and who I felt I needed to be in society. Men particularly feel pressure from society to be the funniest, wealthiest, healthiest, most dependable and most reliable version of themselves at the expense of the real them. Can you be a rich man without wealth? One of my go-to answers to Scarlett, when she asks, 'Dad, Dad, Dad, are we rich? Are we rich?' is 'Don't worry about that, be rich in life's experiences.' Another saying I would use a lot, and I quoted at the start of the book also, is: 'Don't just live the full length of your life, live the full width of it too.' I feel I have done this tenfold but I would now add that most important is to live the full depth of it as well. That is, no hiding behind masks, layers of protection. Deal with your hurts, become aware of your drivers, and get honest with yourself and those around you.

In saying that, drive is certainly seen as a positive attribute in society. Not negative at all. But what is it covering up? I feel one of the biggest things that keeps people in drive is that they are afraid to find out if it is the drive doing all the talking or their real selves. 'It's okay, I'm a driven kinda a guy!' Noooo. 'It's okay, I'm just a layer and layer and layer of protection kinda guy!'

What is left of someone when you strip away drive and ambition?

An interesting backdrop I will insert here. On the 24th of January this year – just over 18 months since the diagnosis, we had let ourselves become comfortable with our new life. Sure, as I alluded to above, it was getting harder. I could no longer walk without the aid of Melinda and/or someone else at times, be it one of the girls, Mel's dad, a passer-by if we were caught out. I can still dress myself and do everything else myself but I sleep two to three times a day to be able to just do the basics. Going out takes military precision with a lot of contingencies. But we had become comfortable with this and we were loving the beautiful intimacy that a terminal illness asks of people. Life consisted of quarterly MRIs, a follow-up chat with the oncology professor and at times a chat with the palliative care team or the neurologist. We were otherwise out of the habit of being in the medical system, unlike when doing regular chemotherapy.

In a funny twist, life on chemotherapy means that you are in the active treatment phase and very much in the medical system. I could walk at this time, almost drive and going out was easier, but appointments ruled our lives and then there was the ghastly fatigue you get from a week of being on chemo that nearly took the whole three weeks to get over before the next lot was given. I stopped active treatment in June after a period of being very unwell with not just one cold but two. My scans were also stable, if not showing signs of improvement which is unheard of in those with a GBM, so after almost a full year of treatment I hung up my boots.

I always went into some kind of reflection around scan time. People would ask me, was I nervous, was I this or that, etc? I would answer, 'No,' but to be honest, I do shift gears a bit. As the stable scans came in, there was a surety that the so-called 'bad scan' was getting closer. My reasoning for saying this is that very few people live 10 years with this particular cancer, so that makes a total of 40 scans (i.e., four scans/year) if you are going to live that long – so essentially you are counting down from 40. I think I got to about eight. The girls on cue asked us this time around, 'Is this one going to be okay?' To which we replied, 'We just don't know.' What we do know is that there are also not many people who last much longer than 18 months, so it was coming and it did. Mel noticed on the telehealth call with the professor that he went straight to asking about symptoms. I had none other than what had happened in December, but this did not relate to what he was about to tell us. Apparently, a new tumour had emerged, this time in the right parietal lobe which is more about speech coordination and any deficit would have been seen on my left side, but it was my right side that I couldn't use as well. Basic neurology here, the left-hand side of the brain mostly controls the right side of the body and the right-hand side of the brain controls the left. We were given options and I admit we went into a spin! For the second time, my life as I knew it and for those around me was set to change forever again.

What has transpired since then is a wait-and-see approach as Melinda and I found ourselves reluctant to go back in for more surgery and/or further chemotherapy due to my already weakened state. As mentioned, I was the fittest, healthiest and strongest both mentally and physically that I had been in my life when going in the first time. I now find myself at my weakest, at least physically that is, as mentally I have become stronger still.

When is it time to pull up the drawbridge and prepare for the end? The old quality of life versus quantity debate. I don't want to be fighting till the end. I want to feel these last months, to complete this life in full presence and prepare for my next life. Remember I mentioned in earlier chapters that maybe my next life I could be a professional snowboarder or racing-car driver? Just jokes, but I do want to pass over in the best way with no regrets from this life, clear my karma so to speak, to be the best I can be in my next life for all, not just for me and mine.

Interestingly enough, as one gets closer to passing over, the more alive you feel. It brings life into sharp focus. Not one of clutching for time but that every day is simply that, every day.

However, after all this, have I renounced going into drive? Have I anything else to prove? It would seem I do. Life would have one more trick up its sleeve. Here I am, nearly at the completion of my book and out of nowhere comes the opportunity to get it published commercially. Having had many a phone call to publishers in the last year or so, I decided that the self-publishing route was the most realistic. Also, I liked the idea of a digital book so that my network overseas had easy access. There was also talk of making it into an audiobook for those with advancing brain cancer who are unable to read anymore due to issues with their concentration or eyesight for that matter. But in came the opportunity. All of sudden my old habits of driving through a project came flooding back. It took me out, and I had to press pause and reassess, what have these last 18 months been about? What are the lessons I've learnt? Did I want to dive back into drive? The answer was no. So here I am, finishing the book. How the next phases will pan out, I don't know; but I do know, I will do it one step at a time and I will do it listening to my inner self, my inner essence, so I can be in the flow of life in my last year of life and not in the same momentum that I lived a lot of the first 50.

So, who am I? Do I actually know now? Well, after writing this book, it certainly isn't who I thought I was.

One thing is for certain, it's been a joy to write it. I recently sent a chapter of the book to someone who commented that it was great my outgoing personality naturally came through from the beginning. That's to miss the point entirely. My outgoing personality came out as a result of my lived experience at a young age. A manufactured fake version of Phil, if you like, that was as a direct result of or reaction to the way I was brought up, not the other way around. I totally get it: it's an easy mistake to make. Heavens, I made the mistake for close to 50 years. Think cause and effect. The two aren't mutually exclusive. I created the outgoing Phil to fill the lack of love I experienced in my childhood. An artificial persona that meant I would get the compliments and adoration that I so desperately wanted. It just so happened I got so good at it that I even convinced myself it was actually me.

This book has been about what I thought life was about: proving yourself – financially, getting the desired recognition, success in relationships, right up to proving I could write and publish a book, all with terminal brain cancer. Yes, it would seem my drive was with me to the end!

What does it mean to have had a good life? Ask 100 people that question and you will get 100 different answers but invariably there will be a common thread and that is money, a trap I fell into. What do I believe a good life is now, given I have months to live not years?

A good life for me is simply waking up in the morning, kissing my partner and kissing my kids.

As mentioned, it was an absolute pleasure to write this book and certainly not a burden ... perhaps because I wasn't setting out to prove anything. **XX**

Afterword

As per my first chapter – given that my life is at the end – I bet you are all 'dying' to know what I have chosen as my funeral song. It is 'We Are All Made of Stars' by Moby – but to celebrate I have also chosen Ronan Keating's 'Life is a Rollercoaster' ... cheesy, you might say if you are Australian, but if you are British, you'll know it is an outright anthem!

I have just completed the book, my first and only ever memoir. Melinda became my scribe for the last two chapters as I didn't have the strength nor coordination to sit at the computer for any meaningful length of time. She also did the first preliminary edit before we sent it off to the professionals yesterday, so she took a deep dive into my life for the second time in her life – having heard it all before in spatterings throughout our relationship. 'Your book is really, really good, Philip,' she would come to bed saying many nights, after staying up to edit it. What she saw was someone who was being driven by a force – that of a man very much trying to prove himself in all facets of life. She can feel it is still in me today, albeit much more surrendered to what the universe is asking of me – now that I have been hit by the bus and am dealing with the consequences of this.

Recall, I called Melinda the unstoppable force and me the immovable object in this time since diagnosis. Well, I suppose I also could be called the unstoppable force throughout my life. Looking back, I didn't stop to really feel what was going on for me; I often reacted to what was happening and moved in that way. That is not to say I was never responsive to the call to change course, as you will have read in the book, but it often took the bricks thrown my way to trip up/over for me to wake up.

It truly is amazing to be in this position to look back at your life and to be looking forward to the next. Am I looking forward to the next? Yes. Am I terrified of how to get there – absolutely fricken terrified! But if what I believe is that there is a next life, then there must have been lives before. And if there were lives before, then I have died many times before. So I've got this! Or my soul has or that bit that is eternal in me.

I have only months to live. I am in the advanced stages of terminal brain cancer.

What is better? The quick unexpected death that comes from a car accident – where the grief is all-encompassing in that moment of shock of the end of someone's life – or the slower process of an expected death that comes with a terminal illness?

Mine is, of course, the latter – we have now had 20 months to live what this is. And even though it has not been a bed of roses, this time has been incredibly worthwhile living. What we as husband and wife with my two girls and our close family and friends have lived has been incredibly enriching. We are all the better for it. There is post-traumatic stress and many who go through this can go into post-traumatic growth. We have definitely grown – all of us. We are all touched and changed from this and I hope there won't be trauma when I go but that my loved ones continue to grow stronger because of what has happened to us.

I mentioned in my earlier chapters that there is a strange comfort in knowing how you will peg out. I still maintain this. It is surreal – and Melinda right by my side is feeling this, too. Obviously, she cannot feel my panic that arises at times in the deepest, darkest parts of the night but she is there and she also feels the whole process is surreal. Normal life is happening around us as we prepare for the biggest journey I will take in this life. We are getting my bags packed, so to speak. Interestingly, a friend who is a palliative care nurse often uses this analogy with her patients as they look at all the things you need to get in order. But it is not just the physical things that you need to attend to, it is the psychological that also need attending to. For me this is more about existential things – I need to surrender to the process, not battle with what is going on.

I am moving on, my loved ones are staying put. Will I be around for them once I go? I have spoken to many people from different walks of life who have lost loved ones early, and for the most part they can still feel them and of course there are symbols like animals, often birds, that confirm they have passed on but also are there with them from time to time.

To follow on from where I left off in the last chapter – the wait and see approach. I just had two scans back-to-back yesterday: one for my brain to check whether the new growth had indeed continued to grow, as it could be radiation necrosis where the brain is still undergoing changes from my whole brain radiation from 18 months ago – and one for my spine to check if a tumour had started growing down there, given my inability to walk.

To keep with the surrealness (not even a real word!) of where we are at, we presented at COBLH (Chris O'Brien Lifehouse) where I normally have my scans and appointments and sure enough, we were told both scans were being performed at RPAH (Royal

Prince Alfred Hospital) across the road – they didn't have room at Lifehouse MRI for the double scan, so we were booked in there at the last minute. Good thing we have learnt to come early for these scans as we had time to reverse out of there – wait for lifts to ground and zoom over to RPA without Melinda losing her precious load, driving me in my wheelchair. Now that is surrendering – letting your partner push you in a wheelchair at pace across busy roads in Camperdown in the Inner West of Sydney and literally running you down the corridors of RPAH to land at our destination of their MRI department, spot on time!

Lifehouse is bustling always when we go for scans but here at lunchtime on a Friday, the smaller set up at RPA was just us in the reception and waiting room. They had our paperwork ready and in no time I was being helped onto the very hard MRI table, ready for a double brain and spine scan. Melinda went for a cuppa at a local café and continued to finish editing the book while I laid there in the MRI with the deafening magnet doing its thing for over an hour. They normally last half an hour or so, so this was a big one – but I think I fell asleep by the end of it as my brain and noise don't mix; it all becomes too much and I go into shut-down mode, a bit like when your mobile phone gets too hot.

We had enough time after this for a quick pit stop and get a large decaf soy cappuccino to go for me. We went back over to the Lifehouse and up the lift to see Dr Brindha Shivalingam – my brain surgeon. Again, the normally bustling shared space of the doctors' clinics on the second floor were all but abandoned and we didn't have to wait long before Brindha and her resident came down from the wards to see us.

What followed was one of the most beautiful and serene doctor's appointments we have ever witnessed. Let me preface this with the fact that Brindha is a saint! She communicates with her eyes and presents with such grace and ease. We were so, so blessed that when I presented to RPA in July 2021, it was Brindha who was on the phone to her registrar guiding the process and we were able to meet her the next day at Lifehouse as she planned with us our next steps. She has been there from the start and she will be with us right to the very end and beyond, as in this session she gladly accepted our offer to hand my brain to her for research.

That is, in the near hour-long session, we looked at the scans – spine clear except for what Melinda of course picked up, which was that over my years of putting my body through the wringer, my lowest lumbar disc was nearly non-existent. I had completely worn it out and it was black on the scan.

My brain: the area for growth had doubled in size in the last seven weeks and the swelling with it, which would explain my increasing fatigue and the fact that I can't really feel my left lower lip anymore. It makes eating interesting. What is also happening are the effects of whole brain radiation 18 months on – there is a cloud across a lot of my brain, so where the sprinklings of tumours were initially like the milky way in the sky, they are now covered by a cloud. In the early days we could see that they were brought under control with the initial treatment through stable scans i.e., no growth, but now we can no longer see what they are doing. It is this cloud change and maybe some changes under these clouds that we can't see that are most probably responsible for my step-wise regression over the last year in not being able to walk – can't really separate the two, it would seem. That is, they don't give whole brain radiation to people thinking they are going to last more than 12 months – as the effect of whole brain radiation is firstly that the effectiveness of the radiation wears off in this time and secondly, the brain changes start to become debilitating. But on the face of it, they go ahead with it as it is effective in buying early good-quality time for people with widespread brain cancer, which is what I had. There is obviously so much we don't know here but this is what we have gleaned.

We could have brain surgery but it would likely give me only a month or two more, alongside chemo that would give me the same – so three months more – and we are just kicking the proverbial can down the road. Also, there are risks of where this tumour is – I could lose the use of my left hand and arm; it is my dominant hand and I have the use of it now and I am independent because of it. I lose this and that all important quality of life goes. Then there is the subject of operating on brain tissue that has been radiated and the recovery is not as good ... that is to say, when the brain tissue is healthy it is like cutting into crème brulée, whereas when the brain has been radiated, particularly in whole brain radiation, there is a resistance to it that just wasn't there before.

After turning over all the information and asking many questions and discussing options, our meeting came to a natural conclusion. We hugged this most gorgeous of human beings and she expressed how impressed she was with how we have been throughout this whole time and of course in these last two meetings.

Upon leaving Lifehouse yesterday afternoon, a thought crossed both our minds: is this the end? We may not be coming back here.

One more stop though, and that is a telehealth with the Prof. He has also been with us from the start. His grace and ease with explaining our various choices with all things oncology is also up there with Brindha. Super steady and answering every question we have had. We will meet with him to decide if low-dose chemo will be of any benefit, considering again the debate between quality of life in these last months and quantity, given the side-effects of chemotherapy and its efficacy in these later stages. That is in Brindha's words: my brain isn't happy and my tumour/s is/are angry!

Is a low-dose chemo just going to stir up my unhappy brain and is the tumour or are the tumours (remember we don't know what is under the cloud) just going to laugh at our last-ditch attempts? Another option is Avastin, which apparently affects the tumour's ability to develop vascular networks for itself – again, it hasn't been shown to be super effective but it may just calm down some of the swelling associated with this new growth. Dexamethasone is a big steroidal anti-inflammatory that is used in cancer treatment to do this latter job but for those of you who have ever come into contact with this one, you'll know that it completely wires you. I had it at the start of my treatment in 2021 and I took some the other day to help me get to an event I wanted to go to; sleep that night was simply out of the question. A nod to just how sensitive my system has become.

I'm sure I will fill you in and I have a suspicion there will be the afterword written here and then the after-afterword written by Melinda; so for that – I love yous all, and always will – all my love forever,

Philip Richard Hills

Coming in to land ...

I RECENTLY DID A LinkedIn post likening my impending end of life to preparing to land a plane. It went like this:

'Bing bong. This is your captain speaking. On the flight deck alongside me is my co-pilot, Melinda Luck.

The fasten seatbelt sign is now on. We are encountering some turbulence and revising our flight path. The new estimated arrival time at my destination is now three months. Please put your seat in the upright position and fold your tray table. It's been a pleasure to have you onboard with me for this journey and on behalf of Philairways, I hope you all have a safe and pleasant onward life ahead.

Cabin crew, arm doors and cross check.'

How everyone would get off the plane including Melinda before I come in to land is where my analogy falls down a bit but you get the idea that I have been extremely well supported throughout this journey, particularly with Melinda by my side. I could not have done it without all who have been there with us in this time – but the last bit I am going alone, temporally speaking.

To say these last few months have been like a plane coming in to land feels to be a very true analogy, however.

I can feel myself peeling off the layers of this life, letting go of what I once thought was very important and probably was when I was in the living of it. Yes, I am still alive but it is like I am between two destinations. Melinda has felt this too – she often describes these months as coming in to land as the reverse flaps/air brakes come into operation. Slowly, slowly, the momentum of my life is coming to a halt. Melinda, to an extent, is coming with me as we spend the last stages of my life together. She can feel it slowing down. I don't like it when she is not here anymore, so she is spending more and more time with me now and minimal time at work. The gradient with which the plane is coming down is shallow – a much slower process than we both expected along with my medical team and even at times there is an uplift and a circling around at the same altitude. To echo the afterword – it is surreal.

We now have carers coming in every morning from 6.30 to 8.30am so that Melinda can go to work and see a client. She then goes out again mid-morning to see another client and a friend or family member comes over to be with me. Both carers and family and friends have been a godsend. I am never left alone now as I am no longer independent with any activities of daily living. I sleep three times a day and over 10 hours each night – my plane is coming in to land.

The tumour is growing. I can't really use my left hand nor the left side of my face and I now smile in a lopsided way! Eating can be a challenge at times too, as well as talking.

Do I get frustrated? Absolutely, but then I realise how useless this is and surrender back to my plane coming in to land. There is a reason why I am still here, so I will live each moment with as much quality as I can.

Am I still terrified? Not anymore. I don't want to be alone and luckily I am not, so I am settled, content. It is funny, when I was first diagnosed there is no way I would have left a tumour to run rampant in my brain and now there is and I am letting it run rampant. It isn't or hasn't been that scary after all. Sure, it isn't great losing function but I am in the dying process. The plane has to drop altitude to land.

And just as the plane needs to prepare for landing, so do we for our final last moments. It is a truly grand process that is taking care of itself; our preparation is to let go and simply to allow. I am, and those around me are, being prepared physically, mentally and emotionally. The process, even though still very surreal, is amazing to bear witness to.

So what did happen a few months ago – did I go with further medical treatment? The big answer is no. It was very clear to me that my body and I needed to do this alone. That is not completely true as with the brain being angry and unsettled, more seizures came so I have had to up my dose of anti-seizure medications, which also make me very tired. This, along with the effect of the tumour and swelling, accounts physically for the many hours I spend asleep or resting. Thankfully, I was able to lower my doses of anti-seizure medication over the last year prior to the new tumour arriving in January, so I have a lot of scope to increase them again to keep the seizures at bay.

As for my funeral songs – I've already played them! We had a 'Celebration of Life – While I am Still Here' a month ago. When Melinda chatted with prospective funeral directors, the idea of saying goodbye to me after I went seemed quite ludicrous considering we could do that while I was still here, so we got together over 70 people within a week at a local bowling club one Friday morning. Melinda and I sat with the girls as she delivered a eulogy of sorts, with me playfully budding in at various times – it was a lot of fun and at the same time of course very sad but so, so good to say what I wanted to say to all those that came. We also had a close English friend of ours, Lucy, read the last chapter of my book as a way of bookending the proceedings so to speak, but also to allow people to understand where I have been and where I am at on the last furlong on the racetrack of life.

I did a podcast with Lucy the year before – 'Hiding Behind a Mask' (Stay in the Loop with Lucy) – which was a great unfolding experience at the time as we took a look at my motivations for writing this book but also a look behind my motivation in life and how they seemingly created the persona that is Philip Hills. You can look that up separately but a lovely segue that came from this was the inspiration for Lyla, my youngest, to write something for my book and here it is:

Life will be much different without Dad and I am going to miss Dad and I know that Mel and Scarlett will miss Dad too and I know people have gone through the same thing and I know cancer is really, really, really scary.

I am going to miss my dad; he has been so amazing throughout this year. He has grown up to be the best dad he can.

Through this year and when he used to pick us up from school, he would tell funny jokes.

Let me tell you one of the jokes my dad told me, let's go!!!

Why did the cow cross the road ... to get to Moooooovies!!!

I am going to miss him.

Lyla Hills

In fact, she read this out at the end of the ceremony.

It was simply a divine and beautiful gathering of my nearest and dearest – a beautiful occasion.

We called our gathering a celebration rather than a goodbye as I was clearly still here but also because I am not going anywhere – I'm coming back! ☺

Planes take off again.

Surrender – Melinda's perspective

THE IDEA THAT you have to fight cancer, battle with it, strive and achieve in this illness has all been debunked as I have witnessed and walked this path with Philip.

If you asked me two years ago, how would you go if your partner was diagnosed with terminal brain cancer, that within eight weeks of diagnosis he would be fully reliant on you and nursing staff in hospital for just about his every move, that he would be in a wheelchair when he came out, using a commode to shower and toilet and that he would be able to walk again but not for very much longer and eventually need a wheelchair full-time until he eventually passes ... I would have said lay down misères – no way – couldn't cope with that. In saying that, whenever Philip expressed his concern that I would not be able to cope if something really big happened in our lives, I always answered with absolute certainty, that yes, I would be able to.

In my background as a physiotherapist, where I have helped countless people recover from injury and chronic pain, there is one area I shied away from and that was neurological rehab. I would say that one of my biggest fears was having a loved one not be able to move due to some neurological condition or injury. Bam – all of a sudden, I was living it. But of course, you can't take in all of the above in one go. That is not what it is about. But you can take bite-size pieces of 'all of that' in the form of one foot in front of the other, then the other and so on. The moment you let your mind and body move ahead of that – gone!

A good friend, who helped us in the early stages and throughout, likened this to being in the eye of the storm. Everything is calm and comes into sharp focus in the eye of the storm – stay here moment to moment, he said; take a step outward and you will be buffeted by the raging torrents of the storm. And as much as we could, we heeded this sage advice. When overcome with emotion, we would check ourselves and say, 'Hang on – we are in the storm – come back into the eye.' A saying we used in those early days was 'day by day' and at the height of Philip's extended hospital stay it was reduced to 'hour by hour'.

So how did I feel on the eve of Philip's release from hospital with him still being very reliant on the supportive surrounds that a hospital room provides, as I dutifully ordered the wheelchair, commode, bed railing and other such supports the occupational therapist advised us to get? Horrible! I didn't want this for my gorgeous, young, fit and amazing man, Philip, but where does it get you, reacting to that, jumping up and down and saying, 'Noooo, this is not what I want to do?' Nowhere. Except into struggle and fight. I rang the various suppliers and placed orders including online for a camping wee bottle. The next day, as I accepted delivery of these items – still hating that this was happening but putting one foot in front of the other – in came the supports for Philip. The commode was not right so we had to send that back and get the suitably sized one. So, for a while in our front courtyard sat a commode chair awaiting pick-up and then a new one sat in its place as I was at work during this change-over period. Confronting, to say the least, and then the next hurdle was getting Philip home. I said I'd come and get him but I was overridden by the hospital medical team who said Philip should come home via ambulance to best support him. He was still having regular seizures, so yep, okay, surrender to that. Confronting again, as my beloved is stretchered from an ambulance, all strapped in, from the street to our front gate. I met them with his newly delivered wheelchair and wheeled him across the threshold – 'HOME, darling, you are home!' The sweetest, most beautiful moment that took away any weird feeling I had about any of the supports I had just ordered. They were in place for our beautiful man to come home after such a long and hugely taxing but transformative time.

But then there was the learning to walk again and eventually we started going out a bit for little walks. Now Philip at this stage had tufts of hair left over from radiation that I had learnt to fashion into a 'Peaky Blinders' (a Netflix series set in the 1920s) hairdo with clippers. To go with this was his ungainly but sort of functional walking style – I was keenly aware of all the onlookers as we made our way. I learnt to stay in the eye of the storm and be completely present with the task at hand, and that was being with my gorgeous, beautiful man who would soon become my gorgeous, beautiful husband. The love, intimacy and connection between us grew exponentially in this time. Sure, the challenges were there but wow – from the initial weekend in hospital where what was in front of us was laid bare, where we absolutely confirmed and deepened our love and commitment to each other in the unfolding days, weeks, months and now years – the growth of us in union together has been otherworldly. I marvel at it, we marvel at it. We actually would not swap out what has happened to us. This illness has healed us both – forever changed.

Surrender it has been. The moment we tried to think our way through situations, try to work it out, we wound ourselves into knots. When we were able to place one foot/wheel in front of the other, the answers to what was next, came to us. Sometimes simultaneously, sometimes not, but we have done this together with of course the enormous help, support and wise counsel from our beautiful family and friends.

Something I will always marvel at is the absolute transformation of the man I know as Philip Hills. He was my gorgeous, super strong, incredibly creative, funny, strikingly handsome, amazing man. Of course, not without his faults as we all have and as you have come to learn from the stories so transparently told throughout this book. He softened, as the layers of protection peeled back. His hugs became like a beautiful warm and loving cloak around you and his absolute love, dedication and appreciation for me and his two daughters became powerfully palpable. He surrendered to what was needed of this illness. He did the treatment regimens until it was time to stop, he took the meds for his seizures and adapted these as the seizures subsided and then recently as they came back again, he did the scans, the various tests required of him. He did it all with grace, integrity and without fight. He put one foot in front of the next, in front of the next.

I can honestly count the number of times Philip did struggle with this illness on one hand. You know, went into a bit of the pity party etc., but it was a quick dip in and a quick dip out. One particular time was when his job was taken away from him. He was able to keep working albeit at a much-reduced level for a year post diagnosis. His company was incredibly supportive until they had to move on and, what felt quite unceremonious for Philip, he found he was gradually without a job. The way this was handled wasn't the greatest in terms of communication which had previously always been free-flowing but had all of a sudden become a bit of a smoke and mirrors affair. He felt this, I felt this too, so it wasn't complete overreaction on

Philip's side but reaction it was. As you have gleaned in the pages of this book and like many men and women for that matter, work was Philip's identity. To have that taken away was raw for Philip but eventually grace and acceptance took over and he surrendered back again to what was unfolding. A huge thing to let go of.

The process of surrender allows other things to surface. Among many things for Philip, one of course was becoming an author and now being published.

The next thing was to sell his beloved classic cars. One by one, in his own time, he did this. Eventually with grace, acceptance, integrity and a profit – go figure: who makes money out of cars!

In these last few months after the recurrence of the GBM, life as we knew it slowed again. It has to, to allow whatever preparation Philip's body has to do to pass over. It has been sad at times, of course. We both have a good grizzle but mostly we hold each other in absolute awe of this otherworldly process. It is otherworldly, as that is where Philip is going. We both share a knowing that once he passes, he goes straight away but that he will be coming back. This isn't a shallow, comforting thing we share between us, but something that is deep and solid. There is joy in this and we are living it.

Acknowledgements

A HUGE THANK YOU to all my family and friends who have supported me throughout my life and particularly in the last two years.

Thank you to Gail for handing me Chris O'Brien's book as I left hospital the first time – it inspired me to put fingers to the keyboard.

Thank you to Simon and Julie for their ongoing inspiration for the book and the divine ongoing support from Rebecca and Natalie throughout.

Thank you to Nick for the beautiful photo shoot you so lovingly put together – you captured my essence effortlessly and Michelle for the gorgeous initial concepts of the book cover design so I could visualise the end product.

Thank you to Gabriele for your precise editing, Désirée for your expert publication guidance and Melinda here too for helping me to finish the book and getting it to publication.

Humongous thank you to my two daughters who have inspired me incredibly in my life.

And to my amazing wife Melinda for literally being there every step of the way in these last two years – I could not have done this without you. You are my rock and guiding light.

To humanity – I love you and will be back for each and every one of you.

Philip Hills